RUSSIA BETWEEN YESTERDAY AND TOMORROW

RUSSIA BETWEEN YESTERDAY AND TOMORROW

Russians Speak Out on Politics, Religion,
Sex, and America

SECOND EDITION

Marika Pruska-Carroll

Véhicule Press

Published with the generous assistance of The Canada Council for the Arts, the
Book Publishing Industry Development Program of the
Department of Canadian Heritage, and the Société de développement des
entreprises culturelles du Québec (SODEC).

Cover design: JW Stewart
All inside photos courtesy of the author
Photo of author (back cover) by Tom Carroll
Set in Adobe Minion by Simon Garamond
Printed by AGMV-Marquis Inc.

CATALOGUING IN PUBLICATION DATA
Pruska-Carroll, Marika
Russia between yesterday and tomorrow / Marika Pruska-Carroll
2nd. ed.

ISBN 1-55065-061-0

1. Russians-Interviews. 2. Russia (Federation)—Social
conditions. 3. Interviews—Russia (Federation) I. Title.

DK510.762.P78 2003   947.086'092'2   C2003

Published by Véhicule Press
P.O.B. 125, Place du Parc Station
Montréal, Québec H2X 4A3

www.vehiculepress.com

Canadian Distribution: LitDistCo 800.591.6250/ orders@litdistco.ca
U.S. Distribution: Independent Publishers Group 800.888.4741
www.ipgbook.com

Printed in Canada on alkaline paper.

Contents

Acknowledgments

Writing *Russia Between Yesterday and Tomorrow* has been a departure from the academic research work I was involved with in the past. Since this book represents my interpretations of Russian views and realities, I take sole responsibility for the book's content.

I wish to thank everyone—friends and strangers—who shared freely and generously their time, opinions and, often enough, their homes and hearts. The Russian people really are hospitable, once they decide they like you. I was fortunate to meet a great many such Russians.

I generallly do not use surnames in the book. People are referred to by their first names only. *Glasnost* or not, most Russians I spoke with preferred it this way. In translating their thoughts and words, I have tried to preserve the distinctiveness of their various speech patterns, reflecting their education, background, and personalities as much as possible.

I want to express my deepest gratitude to my publisher, agent, and editor, Simon Dardick of Véhicule Press, who became interested in the book at an early stage, provided advice and support, and guided me through the editorial process.

I also want to thank Dr. Joan DeBardeleben, Canada's leading expert on Russia and director of the Russian Studies Institute at Carleton University in Ottawa, for her steady support, advice, friendship, and for her faith in my book. Special thanks go to writer Bronwyn Chester for her help and encouragement while editing the early chapters of the manuscript.

My gratitude goes to the Association of Universities and Colleges of Canada and to the Concordia University Part-Time Faculty Association for grants that made it possible for me to make my repeated trips to Russia.

And finally, I want to thank my husband Tom Carroll for his unfailing support, and my son, Marek Carroll, who spent long hours on the computer, transcribing English translations of all my Russian interviews.

Preface to the Second Edition

Russia Between Yesterday and Tomorrow Revisited

I WAS FORTUNATE TO OBSERVE some of the changes underway in Russia as it entered a stage of radical transformation in the early 1990s. Now, with its penchant for the dramatic, Russia is making another major transition. With President Yeltsin's resignation on the eve of the year 2000 and the coming to power of President Putin, post-communist Russia entered its second decade.

In 2002 I visited my old friends and acquaintances and met new ones. Familiar patterns continue to appear, but one major difference was evident right away: life expectancy for Russians is falling. In 1990, the average Russian male lived to age sixty-three. In five years, that figure fell to fifty-seven. By 2002, a generation of middle-aged men that I had met in the 1990s had disappeared. Now the young are more in evidence.

The social, political, cultural and economic concerns that dominated Russia a decade ago have not been resolved. The central question burns with the same intensity now as then: What is the right path for Russia? After years of disappointments, frustration, apathy and cynicism, a new generation still hopes to find answers. They probe such issues as the free market, democracy, freedom and its limits, values, meaning, nationalism and globalism.

But today there is a difference: the young are not in awe of the West, because they are quite familiar with it. What is more, they are not apologetic for the Russian past, the way their parents were, for they don't see themselves as its creators. They are, in fact, quite willing to embrace some of the old symbols, imperial or communist, if they feel they suit Russia today.

These are the people who will form the new Russia in years and decades to come. It is important to understand them and to see Russia through their eyes.

The recognizable quest for new, uniquely Russian paths and the preoccupation with the limits placed on freedom of expression are now accompanied by a puzzling degree of apparent acceptance of President Putin's measures to ensure law and order.

In the early 1990s, Western media sounded the alarm about the danger of totalitarianism returning to Russia. Today, that alarm is being repeated. Then and now I do not consider it a real threat.

I was fortunate in the 1990s to be able to observe, first-hand, a turning point in the destiny of Russia. I am fortunate now to be able to present the Russians, including some whom I met before and who have now emerged as leaders, as they experience a tidal change in their destiny.

Montreal, June 2003

Preface to the First Edition

I SPENT THE SUMMER OF 1991 in Russia researching urban politics. When I returned, my students in Canada greeted me with hundreds of questions about Russia. Although my Russian Politics classes had been large in the year prior to the August 1991 attempted coup, it was this significant event that stimulated intense worldwide interest in Russia. The questions students asked went way beyond normal class material.

Later in the academic year, I asked my students to write down all the questions they would want to ask Russians, if they knew the language and were free to travel anywhere in the country. They took the exercise very seriously and I found myself with over one hundred questions ranging from the abstract, like "What does democracy mean to you?" to the down-to-earth, "Would you ask a man you were about to sleep with for the first time to use a condom, if in fact, you can buy condoms in Russia?"

I made the same request of colleagues and friends and ended up with a list of eighty of the most frequently asked questions. Armed with this list, I spent the summers of 1992, 1993 and 1994 traveling in Russia and talking to the people. I conducted over 150 taped interviews and had numerous untaped conversations with Russians of all walks of life—young and old, rural and urban, blue-collar workers and professionals, students and drop-outs. All conversations and interviews were conducted in Russian and I neither sought nor received any official Russian assistance.

My choice of people to interview was arbitrary. I wandered the streets, universities, shops, galleries, public offices, farms, railroad stations, bus and subway stations, discos, parks and cemeteries. I visited Moscow, St. Petersburg and a number of towns and villages in the European part of Russia—places where my students or acquaintances might go if they had the opportunity.

I picked out faces that looked open to conversation. Some of my interviews developed into friendships which continued throughout my visits. People generously invited me into their homes and often into their hearts, resulting in interviews that frequently went beyond the original scope of my questions. Other encounters lasted only minutes.

Sections of the book overlap; Russians quoted in one section talking about religion, may reappear in another discussing democracy or the economy. Above all, I was intent on preserving natural expression and giving an accurate representation of what I was privileged to hear.

This book is not an academic study. I don't believe this is the time for lengthy social studies of Russia. Events are moving too quickly. What is being lived now in Russia is truly a revolution, the likes of which the country has never seen.

Let me be your guide and translator. Come with me and meet the Russian people.

Montreal, June 1995

Introduction

Now all Russians are free to express themselves. Freedom of expression, that tenet of Western democracy taken so much for granted, is finally a right in Russia. People are no longer afraid to speak. Moreover, they have that essential corollary to freedom of expression: access to information. In my opinion, these rights represent the greatest gain in this period of transition and the greatest hope for the future of Russia. However, nothing can be taken for granted in Russia today because this gain, as the Russians are all too painfully aware, may be lost if it is not closely guarded. Since 1991, ten Russian journalists who were attempting to expose crime and corruption, have been killed in the former Soviet Union; six in the Russian Federation alone. The opportunity that Russians now have to read of major events in the newspapers and to view their coverage on television, would have been unthinkable only a few years ago. The detailed coverage of the war in Chechnya, with its grim and bloody imagery, is a prime example of the unprecedented freedom of the media in Russia.

It is essential to hear what Russians themselves think of the transformations affecting them, because Western journalists and academics all too often mistake the interests of the White House or of the Russian political elite for the interests of the people. Russia's high-level politics, for instance, seems to be of minimal interest to the majority of Russians. Their perception of what is going on in their country is quite different from ours. In general, we in North America tend to be far more optimistic than the Russians.

We like to think that democracy and the free market have prevailed over communism and that the Russians have made their choice. We are led to believe by our media that it is only a handful of hard-liners—neo-fascists led by Vladimir Zhirinovsky, or a group of old people waving red flags and flashing an occasional portrait of Lenin or Stalin—that stand in the way of political and economic progress. The December 1993 elections demonstrated clearly how mistaken a perception this is.

Neither democracy nor a free market economy dominates Russian thinking. Communism and nationalism are not dead. The old Soviet mentality is still vigorous. Russian society is more diverse than ever.

I have observed that the differences in opinion between Russians are not so much between communists and democrats or between conservatives and liberals—these labels don't mean much to Russians; the differences—and they concern nearly every aspect of life, from sexuality to education, from employment to morality—emerge along lines of age, class and gender. It is these differences that so well exemplify the social transformations being experienced in Russia, and it is to these differences that I propose we listen. But before embarking on our walk through Russian cities and the countryside, I wish to issue a few words of caution.

There is a great tendency in the West, and in North America in particular, to judge Russia as if our own parliamentary democracies and free market economics were working perfectly. Such is simply not the case. In nearly every section of the globe there are crises in traditional politics. In Japan, Italy, the United States, France, Great Britain, and Canada, there have been sensational exposures of political corruption, and there is a growing disgust with, and wariness of, the political process. The symptoms of this disaffection are many: low electoral participation, difficulty in recruiting new blood into the established political parties and a general lack of faith in the moral integrity of politicians and in their ability to lead.

There is a notable absence of statesmanship on the international scene. Where are the leaders of nations, trusted and followed, who espouse political programs deeply rooted in popular ideologies? The men and women of the age and status to be leaders seem more interested in technocratic efficiency or media stardom, than in the vocation of politics.

Ideologies are blurring. The traditional understanding of "left" and "right' in politics does not apply in the same way it used to. The complexity of interests of different groups within any country leads to ideological hybridization. One can now be "left wing" in terms of politics and "right wing" in terms of the economy; radical and conservative; democratic and undemocratic; ecologically progressive and ecologically wasteful; idealistic and materialistic. These contradictions apply equally in Russia.

From time to time, an alarm is sounded by the Western media that totalitarianism lurks just around the corner. The vision of black and brown with a touch of red is unfolded. Such a possibility is probably marginal just now, but it cannot be dismissed altogether because both the nationalists and the remaining followers of communism constitute a very strong force in Russia and they can easily be exploited by political leaders. What is immediately apparent, and far more threatening to the new Russian democracy, is the gradual disintegration of organized social life. It is as apparent in the former Soviet republics, as it is in Russia. Institutions still exist but they no longer work. There is a crisis within education, health care and the family. But let us keep in mind that the democratic systems of Western Europe and North America are also experiencing difficulties in adapting to new economic and technological conditions. We are all in a state of a profound transformation. Yet, even as we admit that our political processes and institutions are in transition, we do not hesitate to advocate their adoption by Russia and Eastern and Central Europe. We tend to perceive the former Soviet Empire and its satellites as a homogenous entity and promote identical ways of dealing with their political and economic ills.

While some East Europeans, because of their separate and distinctive political cultures and traditions, will develop patterns mirroring those of Western Europe, some of which may eventually work, Russia is different. Russia's political chaos is unique; the Russia to emerge from this situation will not be a clone of a troubled Western democratic model.

No one can predict what a Russian democracy or Russian post-Communist economy will look like; we don't know what values Russians will adopt. All one can say is that out of the social unrest that reigns in Russia today, individuals—post-Soviet individuals—will emerge as the next generation of leaders. Some will emerge from among the people I have spoken to; others will resist change. Both will form the new Russia, and for this reason it is important to listen to their voices and to see Russia through their eyes.

PART ONE

Personal Experiences and Impressions

Selling flowers on a Moscow street corner. Russians always buy
cut flowers to give to a friend or to bring home. Despite the
dismal state of the economy, flowers are in great demand.

The New and Old Russia

In Russia today, there are clearly two different countries: one is the new, murderously competitive urban Russia of Moscow and St. Petersburg, the other, an unchanged Russia of small towns and countryside.

As a street vendor in his early twenties, a former physics student who left university, put it:

"I see Russia as a forest where the people have become wolves, and in order to survive, we must all be equally ruthless."

And in the small village of Petrovka, only sixty kilometers from Moscow, a forty-two-year-old peasant woman spits on the ground in disgust when asked about the changes in Russia.

"It is all these good-for-nothing city folk. They are destroying everything," she says.

Then there is the Kremlin and its constant stream of black limousines carrying new *vlasti* (power brokers). Valentina Pavlovna, a fifty-five-year-old retired cook, thinks that "these guys in limos are Russia's enemies, paid by the West, probably by the U.S., in order to destroy Russia from the inside."

Urban democrats indulge in endless debates to which few people listen. Leonid Danilovich, a fifty-six-year-old film director and a typical member of the Russian intelligentsia, is glad that communism is gone but does not trust "this army of dyed-in-the-wool democrats."

There is the urban Russia of the railroad stations crammed with countless homeless and dispossessed people. There is the Russia of filth, physical disintegration and ever-increasing crime.

"Look at what they are doing to Moscow!" exclaims Katerina Ivanovna, a retired clerk. "See how filthy, how smelly, how dangerous it has become. Life is so hard now. And everybody is edgy and frustrated. People rob, steal and kill. It is simply a shame. I am a native Muscovite and my heart aches when I see what is happening to the city."

Leonid, a father of two teenage children, is very concerned about crime.

"Travel anywhere, no matter how short the distance, can be dangerous. I continually worry about my children and I'm not talking about the mafia and organized crime. Boys are killing other boys for their shoes or jackets."

This is the new Westernized urban Russia that horrifies most older Russians but to which the younger ones are adapting with alarming speed.

There is the Russia for Western tourists and a handful of natives who have access to the private and foreign shops with their Western prices and Western merchandise. Meanwhile, beggars and starving pensioners line the streets.

A new "colonial" mood is prevalent across Russia. Westerners play the role of the "white masters" and the Russians are the "poor natives." The difference between the buying power of Westerners and that of most Russians is colossal. Westerners seem to be able to buy virtually anything and everything, and all doors are open to them. Russians, unless they have enormous amounts of money, are second-class citizens.

There have never been so many Westerners, with so few restrictions, in Russia, and there has never been such resentment towards them as there is today. There is also a great deal of resentment against the new rich Russians, summed up in especially strong terms by older Russians for whom the word "businessman" is synonymous with the word "crook."

Reality is developing simultaneously on two planes: on the level of economic and political transformations, and on the level of old Russia, deeply rooted in its past. However, the drastic changes in the overall political climate during the past three years have deeply affected the mood of the Russian public.

The people are pessimistic, angry, bitter, resentful and resigned. The bloody dissolution of the Russian Parliament in early October 1993, fractured Russian opinion. Two years later, Russian society is just as divided.

There are basically two social classes in today's Russia: the " new rich" who are former and present *apparatchiks*—many of whom occupy high posts in Yeltsin's government, along with former managers of state enterprises turned capitalist, some of whom are members of the Russian mafia. Combined, they represent about five percent of the population. The other 95 percent are Russians who "have had enough of it all" and who simply want to "live like humans."

In the past, Russians counteracted the grim communist reality with political jokes told in close circles of family and friends. Today, not too many people are in the mood for jokes. The few that are circulating reflect a reality

Waiting for the bus under a poster advertising "West"-brand cigarettes. The text invites us to "escape the humdrum of everyday life."

These two young rapper-style teens on a St. Petersburg street could be from North America or Western Europe.

that is for most Russians even grimmer than the communist one they once experienced.

Nine-year-old Ivan runs to his mother and says, "Mom, something strange is going on. They turned on the electricity, the water is running, and our telephone works!"

"My God!" cries the mother. "The communists are back in power!"

But few find the Russian version of democracy amusing. "Hungry people don't laugh much," one is told.

The growing crime rate and an ineffective police force are sometimes the objects of ridicule. A tourist asks a policeman standing on a street corner, "Is it true that this neighbourhood is very dangerous?"

The policeman responds, "What a crazy question! Would I be here if there was any danger?"

Everybody knows the expression "communism was a fair distribution of poverty, while capitalism is an unfair distribution of wealth," but now the irony reflects the painful edge on the experience of most Russians.

Gorbachev and *perestroika* are not thought of too kindly and a joke that was born in the late 1980s is still making the rounds:

"There were two possible ways to go about *perestroika*, the realistic way and a fantastic one, and Gorbachev failed them both. The realistic way was to bring some intelligent beings from outer space and have them put Russia in order; the fantastic one—to let the Russians do it themselves."

And another one: "Who invented *perestroika*, communists or scientists? Communists. Scientists would have experimented with animals first."

Russian Television

BEFORE *perestroika*, Soviet television was state owned and controlled. There were several channels, all virtually identical and all equally dull, serving the state and expressing its official line.

Today, Russian television is in the process of being privatized. The largest network, Ostankino, is already 50 percent owned by private shareholders. The other half is still held by the state. Its official name as of April 1995 is Russian Public Television and it is practically indistinguishable from Western television. Although Ostankino is governed by rules and regulations, few are followed or obeyed thus far and, if one has the money, one can get all the channels that are accessible in the West. Russian channels copy the style of Western TV and enjoy unrestricted freedom of expression.

It is five p.m. when I turn on the TV in the apartment I have rented. Selecting a channel at random, I see three young, heavily made-up women dressed in white leggings and low-cut exercise outfits in contrasting colors, their white teeth flashing and white legs flying to pulsating rock music. This is an aerobic exercise show for Russian housewives.

I couldn't help but wonder how many women were at home watching such a program. More than likely it's women who have been recently laid off.

I switch to a children's show. A group of young boys and girls dressed in Czarist soldier uniforms and folk dresses are dancing and singing. It is a far cry from the Young Pioneers days when boys and girls dressed in white shirts and red scarves would be singing songs about Lenin and the Revolution.

I continue channel-hopping. A report on the health of children informs me that every fourth baby born in Russia now dies at birth. The infant mortality rate in Russia matches that of the Third World. The program's name turns out to be "Let's Love Children" and it calls for a return to subsidized day-care and nurseries.

Another channel shows a religious pilgrimage. Hundreds of people travel by foot to old Russian monasteries. In the past the faithful would go to seek spiritual advice from the monks who had their receiving hours. This tradition has been restored. On the screen, a Russian Orthodox priest speaks about the meaning of life and death; he describes old Russia's monks and monasteries and the role they played in preserving and developing the culture of Russia. In the background, a choir sings religious songs in Old Church Slavonic, the language of the Russian Orthodoxy. Today, just as before the Revolution, people travel to monasteries to cure their souls.

"The Russian soul is sick these days," says the priest.

"Our old monasteries should play a greater role as spiritual healers."

As he tells how the process has already begun, the camera pans over the assembled pilgrims—young and old, men and women.

Another day I watch a cooking lesson. A man in a large white chef's hat and an apron is demonstrating how to cook healthful and delicious food. He addresses himself to women only. The chef emphasizes how important it is to preserve vitamins and minerals in the preparation of meals.

"Do not overcook," he cautions his viewers. "Eat plenty of fresh fruits and vegetables."

His final creation is a fantasy of color: green, yellow, and red peppers are artistically arranged, thick steaks look juicy and pink, potato pancakes are delicately garnished with parsley and mushrooms. I admire both the culinary creation and the advice and cannot help but wonder to whom this program is addressed. The price of just one pepper, of any color, is ten times more than the price of one big head of cabbage, and one large head of cabbage, with a few bones and potatoes added, provides a soup to feed an entire family.

When I asked Russians what they thought of such cooking lessons, they laughed. Most of them said they like watching cooking shows the same way they enjoy watching "Dynasty" and "Dallas." Others were angry because such shows offended people who had barely enough to eat.

In a TV commercial a Lenin look-alike, replete with Lenin's mannerisms, dictated a revolutionary bulletin to a Trotsky look-alike. The viewer can't really hear the words because of the loud revolutionary songs in the background. As the music fades, we hear Lenin's voice and we discover that it is an appeal to trade stocks!

On the news, there was a report about the exhumation of twenty-six bodies in the Novo-Chekasky district—victims of a mass shooting by the authorities in 1962, during the "free" Khrushchev years. The victims were striking workers. Thirty-two years after their deaths, they are exhumed and then buried with honours.

Another news item documents Alexander Solzhenitsyn's return to Russia after twenty years in exile in Vermont. The famous dissident is shown honouring the graves of 12,000 former prisoners of the Siberian labour camp in Chkabarovsk where he was a prisoner.

On another day I tune into a story about AIDS in Russia. "The danger of AIDS is real. It does exist; it can happen to you," says the anchorman, adding that there is not enough being done to make Russians aware of the danger, and that pretending that there is no problem is not going to make it disappear.

Moving quickly from AIDS to the economy, the anchorman informs viewers that within just one year, prices of most goods went up over 100 percent. "Prices are dictated by the mafia monopoly and not by the market," the anchorman tells us. "They can be expected to rise still further," he adds.

A little later the same channel reports that a newly-opened bank had a complete floor destroyed by fire. There is no question that it was an act of arson, we are told; it happens all the time.

The Boy Scouts of Russia are back for the first time since they were declared illegal in 1926. We watch them marching at a scout camp carrying old, pre-revolutionary flags and icons. A major requirement of a Russian scout is to believe in God and the Russian Orthodox Church. All scout camps and activities are organized around the church.

A few days later, another news item caught my interest. Throughout Russia, the rate of violent crimes in 1994 rose 30 percent. The people interviewed talked about friends and family members who had been murdered in their homes or on the street. The camera zoomed in on the tearful faces of people who had lost relatives and friends.

The next day I turn the TV on to the startling news that yet another member of the legislature has been killed in front of his house. The report indicates that it was a planned assassination.

Recently, there was yet another killing. This time it was thirty-eight year-old Vladislav Listyev, one of Russia's best-loved television personalities who had just been appointed the general director of Russian Public Television. A few weeks earlier, because a handful of individuals monopolized access to television advertising, Listyev announced a ban on advertising on his network. He was murdered in the stairwell of his apartment building. While nobody questions the fact that it was a contract killing, the motive remains unclear.

The diversity and startling honesty of the news and the variety of both Russian and Western programs are indications of the remarkable changes that have occurred in Russian society. The most dramatic example is the way the Chechnya war is being brought to millions of Russian living-rooms, just as the Vietnam War became a daily reality for American viewers three decades earlier. The impact of the explicit, bloody, and violent images of war and destruction is enormous. There is a growing protest movement against the war—something unprecedented in the seventy years of Soviet and Russian history. There is also mounting criticism of Yeltsin and his policy toward Chechnya.

Stairways at Night

MOSCOW AND ST. PETERSBURG used to be exceptionally clean cities. In the early 1980s it was not unusual to be rebuked by passers-by if one dropped a cigarette butt on the street. Now the streets in both cities are dirty, and the prevailing smell is that of rotting garbage and urine, particularly around the subway stations, where, after dark, there is a lot of drinking and fighting.

Small towns I have visited around Moscow over the past three years do not look or smell much better. Russia smells terrible. It is easy to understand why. In apartments and communal rooms, there is a great shortage of space. People use their bathrooms for storage. One can find almost anything in Russian bathtubs—from live carp to buckets of coal or potatoes. The bathroom's usual function is often ignored.

Matters are not helped by a lack of hot water. During the summer, different sections of cities throughout Russia are deprived of hot water for periods ranging from one to five weeks. No one complains or seems to be surprised.

"They're cleaning the system; it's a normal maintenance routine," I was told with resignation by town and city dwellers. So people simply go to public baths or drop in on their friends to use their hot water.

Laundry facilities are virtually nonexistent. It is only recently that a few laundromats and dry cleaners have appeared in large cities. Only about 25 percent of Russians have washing machines and practically nobody has a dryer. Closet space, even in affluent Russian apartments, is sparse, and clothing tends to be stored in piles. Russians seem to be resigned to this situation. Yet the same people who are unable to wash their clothes or take a shower on a regular basis, won't hesitate to spend their weekly paycheck on a ticket to the ballet or the opera.

To cross any major street in Moscow (and some are twelve lanes wide), one must use an underpass. The underpasses are long, dark, often wet and, over the past five years, teeming with human activity. People line the graffiti-covered walls selling everything imaginable. Tables display books—political literature of every nuance and description. Old women sell antiquated household objects, shoes, candles, and candies. Young men hawk jeans, T-shirts, and even toys. Beggars of all ages and some unusual entertainers complete this subterranean scene.

Sweet-voiced children, who ought to be in school, are instead dressed in rags, and perform heart-wrenching musical routines. Once in the underpass I saw an elderly woman with her face covered, singing in an exquisite operatic voice. It was whispered to me that she was an unemployed opera star. On another occasion, an elderly woman wearing a blonde wig, danced bizarrely to the music of a grizzled accordion player. Because a lot of stealing occurs in the underpasses, I had been warned by friends to be very careful.

A pair of strong legs is needed to wander around in Moscow, especially if one ventures off the beaten track. There are no places to sit down. One walks and walks for kilometers without finding a bench, café or restaurant. There are benches in the parks that can seat sixteen people, but first one must find a park.

Moscow is a city of eight million people and approximately 400 restaurants. By comparison, in New York, a city of about ten million people, there are some 28,000 cafés and restaurants. The few restaurants that do exist in Moscow are very expensive even by Western standards. The McDonald's and Pizza Hut restaurants, while cheaper than other places, are not cheap by Russian standards. Six to ten dollars for a meal translates into a week's wages for many Russians.

I observed a scene on Tverskaya Street, Moscow's main street, that left me badly shaken. It was only a few steps from Moscow's first McDonald's. It was five p.m. and a group of Russian teenagers was hanging around. Among them was a girl no more than fifteen years old. She seemed hysterical, throwing herself against one of the boys and making inarticulate noises. She wore blue jeans and a plain T-shirt, and her blonde hair was matted and dirty. It was quite obvious that she was high.

I was horrified when one of the boys took a syringe out of his pocket, and, while two boys held the girl, injected her with something. His eyes were bloodshot; he was in no better shape than she was. While this was happening, passers-by averted their eyes. On a nearby corner two policemen acted with total indifference.

One evening I was excited about going to Taganka, the famous Moscow theatre, with a Russian woman friend of mine. We managed to get the tickets from a well-connected friend—a film director. It was the closing night of Pasternak's "Doctor Zhivago," directed by the celebrated director Lubimov. It was literally the last show because Lubimov was leaving Russia permanently. He now lives

A Moscow street performer.

A typical street market scene around a subway station entrance.
Asians, Georgians, Armenians, and Azerbaijanis predominate.

and works in Paris.

After the show, we began walking toward the subway. It was ten p.m., the evening was warm and I suggested that we walk for a while before taking the subway home. I knew that the streets could be dangerous, but at this hour everything seemed peaceful. My friend was not enthusiastic but she gave in and we began to walk.

A few streets from the theatre, still in the centre of town, we realized with a touch of panic that we were the only people on the street. There were, however, a number of cars parked along the sidewalks and I was surprised to discover that each car was full of men, just sitting there in the darkness. My friend became quite alarmed. She told me they were *chernota*, which is a derogatory term used to describe dark complexioned people mostly from the former Soviet Asian and Caucasian republics and in popular view often linked with organized crime or the mafia. She was anxious to end our walk.

When I asked her why she thought these men were connected with the mafia she didn't have an answer. All she said was, that by the look of them, they were clearly from the former Asiatic republics. That was apparently enough to indicate their evil intent and affiliations. As we approached the subway station, we attracted the unwelcome attention of a large group of mean-looking young toughs—obviously under the heavy influence of alcohol or drugs. We ran past them, nearly tripping over piles of garbage from the food kiosks—some more than a meter high, with rats and mice scurrying about.

We made it to the subway and were fortunate there were enough people around to make us feel more at ease. The Moscow metro is still remarkably efficient and safe, and its striking architecture never fails to make an impression. Despite the deterioration of services throughout the city, the authorities manage to keep it quite clean.

I got off at my station, alone at a half-past eleven. Outside the subway, drunk men were lurking in the shadows. I knew that walking these few streets home was not going to be fun. At that time, in the summer of 1993, I lived near Moscow University in a middle-class district where most people live in six-storey high apartment blocks built about three decades ago. The apartment where I was staying belonged to a typical member of the Russian intelligentsia. The walls were lined with an incredible number of books, paintings and photographs—all looking crowded and a bit worn. The place wasn't dirty but the sheer volume of things in such a small space made it difficult to keep it tidy. I rented the apartment from the mother of a friend. She was the widow of a well-known poet. To make ends meet, she would occasionally rent her apartment to foreigners for U.S. dollars. While the apartment was rented, she lived with her divorced daughter.

The apartment buildings are situated on wide streets divided by islands of trees running the length of the street. Although only twenty meters wide, the island serves as a park, with benches along the way. I had to cross through the trees, mostly birches planted twenty years ago. The same Russian birches that looked so attractive during the day assumed a sinister appearance at night. Somewhere I could hear the rowdy voices of drunken men. I ran as quickly as I could.

I had been at this address for only two days and I wasn't familiar with the neighbourhood. All the buildings look identical even during the day. There were few street lights and most street numbers were missing and I could not find my building.

Each apartment complex has a street number and six to eight entrances, each numbered separately. The fact that practically all the entrance lights had been broken or stolen, did not help. After half an hour of circling around trying to decipher entrance numbers with a match, I found mine. In total darkness, I ran up the stairway to the fifth-floor apartment. On the second floor, I tripped over a sleeping body.

There are elevators, but I wouldn't dream of using one. About the size of a refrigerator, dimly-lit and frequently used as urinals, they often get stuck between floors. It wasn't easy to find the keyhole in the dark, but the sweet moment came, and with great relief I found myself safely behind the closed door of my apartment.

Security

BECAUSE OF MY CONCERN FOR SAFETY, the following year, in the summer of 1994, I rented an apartment in what is probably the most elegant section of Moscow. I lived on Kutuzovsky Prospect, next door to the apartment building where Brezhnev and the other Soviet elite used to have their city apartments. No longer did I have to worry about night-time subway expeditions—I had a trolley bus stop directly in front of my building and no taxi would refuse to take me to such a respectable location.

Kutuzovsky Prospect, one of Moscow's main avenues, is twelve lanes wide. A pedestrian has to walk at least a kilometer in either direction to locate an underpass.

A beautiful, elaborately-embellished 17th-century house, now abandoned,
in an old part of Moscow.

I experienced a privileged aspect of the city dweller's life. All my neighbours were affluent. Everybody in Moscow was worried about crime but the degree of fear was in direct proportion to a person's wealth. The more one has, the more one worries, and the more one attempts to protect his possessions. Home security insurance in Russia is a booming business.

My landlord was a fifty-six-year-old accountant, working for an icon and antique store. She was twice married, with two adult daughters who were married and living elsewhere. She had a wonderful icon collection and valuable oil paintings by noted Russian artists. Her large two-bedroom apartment was impressive by any standards, with bay windows, hardwood floors, high ceilings, antique carpets, a piano, and an art nouveau fireplace.

There was no lack of appliances—two Sony TV sets, a VCR, a sophisticated telephone, and every imaginable gadget in the kitchen and bathroom. There was every evidence of wealth in her full closets and stylish Victorian bedroom. There were lights on in the stairways day and night and nobody slept or urinated in the landings. My hostess, like her neighbours, had good reason to fear that her possessions might be irresistible to someone. Apartment break-ins, especially in this neighbourhood, are the work of organized crime. In some cases, it is mafia perpetrating crimes agains other mafia members.

Outside, these buildings look officious. They were built in the 1930s specifically for the Red elite and they are quite different from the standard fare that was put up for ordinary Russians. Today, the apartments are bought by the new elite: bankers (one was recently shot in front of his door), the mafia, old-time *apparatchiks*, who have made their way into the new elites, movie stars and directors and, of course, those who work for joint ventures and are well paid in Western currencies. The mafia, who appear most respectable, worry a lot about being preyed upon by other organized crime elements. All of these apartment-dwellers have property they want protected.

My hostess, like everybody else in the building, has three metal doors leading to her apartment. In addition, the whole place is wired and hooked up to a security system which is elaborate and expensive to install and maintain.

While I certainly felt safe inside this fortress, more than once I became nervous while operating the system. I had to learn the process of turning the system on and off within the prescribed time limit whenever I left the apartment and every time I returned. On one occasion, I made an error with the numbers and passwords. The security people appeared in full force with their guns drawn. This incident cost me the equivalent of ten dollars in fines and an hour explaining myself.

Shopping in Moscow

I NEEDED TO BUY BREAD. Canadian honey, Dutch cheese and German milk are available in private stores that charge high prices for these imported products. Honey, cheese, and milk are unobtainable in state stores because it is no longer profitable for Russians to produce them. Bread is one of the Russian-made products you can still purchase in a state-run store, but I had not been able to find bread anywhere for two days.

I could easily have purchased American cigarettes, French perfume, or roses from Georgia, just around the corner from my house. Or I could buy kiwi fruit and bananas, all at exorbitant prices, of course—but no bread. These products are sold in a variety of ways. Sometimes they are spread out on the sidewalks or sold by individuals from folding stands. There are also semi-permanent kiosks which are frequently burned to the ground by the competition. If you have the time you can do your shopping at one of the many open markets.

One day I complained to a neighbour that I couldn't find bread anywhere. Without a moment's hesitation, she took me by the hand to her own apartment and insisted on giving me half a loaf.

This is an amazing quality of the Russian people. Now, more than ever, they act indifferent at best and hostile at worst, toward strangers, Russians or foreigners. However, once they decide to accept you as one of their own, they embrace you totally and are willing to go to any length to be warm and accommodating. And given how difficult it is to obtain most products, not to mention the expense, their willingness to share is astonishing.

Foreigners who visit Moscow, St. Petersburg and other large cities in Russia, often have the impression that consumer goods are readily available. While it is true that one can buy many things if price is no object, it is not a reality experienced by most Russians. Few can shop in stores carrying foreign goods because the prices are simply too high. Foreigners, as a rule, don't have to prepare meals for themselves since they usually eat in restaurants, so they don't experience the frustrations related to shopping in Russia. More often

Opulence on display in Moscow. In this heavily-guarded Austrian store specializing in silver, crystal and china, the least expensive item costs U.S.$30—an amount some pensioners have to live on for a month.

Woman begging outside an exclusive boutique. She could be
a pensioner who cannot survive on her pension.

than not, tourists shop for gifts and see a variety of merchandise similar to that displayed in shop windows in the West. Consequently, foreign visitors hail the success of the reforms which have resulted in this apparent abundance of goods.

The first thing one observes in these new-style stores is the presence of security personnel. The more elegant the store, the more numerous the heavily-armed young men, dressed in navy jackets and grey pants, guarding silk suits, American whisky, silver, porcelain, and cigarettes.

There is one aspect that all stores in the city share. Whether you enter a dingy and crowded state store, or one of the opulent, empty, and guarded private stores, you are met with the same curious combination of suspicion and indifference by the sales personnel. Don't bother asking questions about a product because the only reaction will be one of surprise or hostility. In fact, the sales staff will likely view questions as a personal affront. Press the issue and it will get you absolutely nowhere.

Service is poor because the concept of service is foreign to Russians. During the years of Soviet power, there were always shortages of goods and nobody had to court the customer; customers tried to earn the goodwill of the sales staff because it was the only way to obtain scarce goods. As a result, a position in sales was a desirable one. It provided opportunities for extra earnings, not always honest, and it gave one a sense of power. This mentality still persists though the circumstances have changed. Furthermore, since wages for the sales staff are low, there is no incentive for kindness and good manners. "Service with a smile" as taught and practiced in Western retail outlets, is something still new to sales people and customers in Russia.

One day I needed to buy a subway map but I couldn't find one. Finally, one street vendor advised me to buy a T-shirt with a metro map on it. "This way," he said, "you not only will have a map, you will also get to wear it." Needless to say, I jumped at the opportunity, so that stranger seen in the Moscow metro spreading a T-shirt on the wall to figure out where she was going, was me.

The Writer's Return

WHEN NOBEL PRIZE WINNER Alexander Solzhenitsyn returned to Russia in 1995, after twenty years of exile in the U.S.A., he expressed the hope that he could "be at least of some help" to Russia. But he received only a lukewarm welcome.

With money earned in the West, Solzhenitsyn bought land on the outskirts of Moscow in the village of Troyce-Lykovo and built a large mansion there. That act alone set him apart from his peasant neighbours and placed him in the same category as some other inhabitants of the village: the mafia and the former, still privileged communists who are the objects of his scorn and criticism.

They, like Solzhenitsyn, live behind tall fences in very large houses and estates. For the neighbouring peasants, they might be from another world altogether. In 1956 the writer exposed Stalin's forced labour camps in the literary journal, *Novy Mir*. It eventually appeared in his remarkable 1962 book, *One Day in the Life of Ivan Denisovich*. Solzhenitsyn found that his compatriots no longer seemed interested in listening to him.

Solzhenitsyn was an unquestionable hero in 1956. People would pay an equivalent of their monthly salary to buy a copy of the *Novy Mir* literary journal where his book was published. Today, young people don't even known his name and the older ones have mixed feelings about their former hero.

The word in the literary journals is that Solzhenitsyn has became a stranger to the new capitalist Russia. There are still those among the Russian population who view him as a prophet, but many consider him a reactionary and the enemy of democracy.

Most of the Russian intelligentsia consider his views to be anachronistic. Liberals and democrats alike consider Solzhenitsyn very foreign to the Russia of reforms and democracy, and they believe he is a dangerous carrier of outdated longings.

Solzhenitsyn, on the other hand, says that there are no real democrats in Russia and those who call themselves democrats, Yeltsin included, are in fact nothing but "communist pretenders" who "poison the spiritual air of Russia."

It is interesting, note Russian newspapers, that Andrei Sakharov, the father of the Russian nuclear bomb and another famous Russian dissident, never saw eye-to-eye with Solzhenitsyn. Elena Bonner, wife of the late Sakharov, who took her husband's place as a champion of democracy and human rights, has remained silent about Solzhenitsyn's return. According to the papers, her silence speaks volumes.

The mass media treat Solzhenitsyn with, at worst, a mixture of sarcasm

In his old-style soldier's greatcoat, this old man calls to mind
pre-revolutionary Russia, as he poses for tips from tourists.

The author in front of St. Basil's Church on Red Square.
This jewel of Russian architecture was built by Ivan the Terrible
who blinded the architects after they finished so they could never
build anything like it again. In recent years, churches are being restored,
and new churches built, all across Russia.

and scorn, and at best, with indifference. One gets the impression that he is simply burdensome because his ideas glorifying the czarist past are so distant from those held by present-day progressive Russians.

It is a sad paradox, but Solzhenitsyn, who in 1956 was first and foremost an anti-communist, is now said to sound like a communist. He has made numerous statements criticizing Russia's attempts at democracy and he is against privatization. He openly criticizes Yeltsin and his reforms.

Curiously, he is attacked by both the Russian left and the right. Zhirinovsky advised Solzhenitsyn to go back to America, saying: "We don't need immigrants who for twenty years were lying about us to our enemies."

Indeed, Solzhenitsyn returned to his native country to find a great many contradictions and paradoxes—shameless wealth side-by-side with poverty, and chaos and anarchy with strong authoritarian elements.

The seventy-five-year-old writer clearly envisioned himself a spiritual leader of Russia, one who would restore and revive Russian Slavophile traditions. In this vein, he called for the restoration of the Russian empire, an empire made up of Slavs for Slavs. He insists that Russia doesn't need the West to be reborn. He talks about the Russian soul, return "to the people" and "to the soil." He believes that a return to the land and agrarian values is the way for Russia to emerge from the present crisis.

For Solzhenitsyn, the free market will result in Russia selling-out to the West, and democracy and will lead to anarchy and destruction. He is very concerned about the twenty-five million Russians still remaining in the former Soviet republics. Because of this concern, he seems to be of use to some nationalists. But even they are reluctant to embrace yesterday's anti-communist hero. If Solzhenitsyn receives some minimal recognition for what he accomplished in the past and for what he represents today, it will be in the provinces where change takes place at a slower rate.

Solzhenitsyn's puritanism is expressed in his disdain for feminism and any alternative lifestyle. His religious tolerance includes only the Russian Orthodox faith.

Church boutiquess like this in central Moscow (and elsewhere) have not beeen seen in the city since pre-revolutionary days.

PART TWO

People and Values

Just a Family

OVER THE PAST THREE YEARS I have become good friends with a Moscow family. I always look forward to seeing Ivan and Tatyana, both in their fifties, and their sons Ilya and Grisha. Ivan is a sociologist and a member of the Russian Academy of Science; Tatyana is a retired scientist.

Ilya holds a master's degree in sociology, and is married to a dentist. He and his wife are in their mid-twenties. They have a four-year-old daughter. Ilya recently began to work for a joint venture-company and is very pleased with the changes taking place in Russia. He was able to get his job chiefly because of his fluent command of English. Two years ago, he spent a semester in the United States as an exchange student at Penn State University. Ilya and his family live in a small, one-bedroom apartment.

Grisha is thirty years old and is employed as a skilled worker in a Moscow tool factory. He still lives at home with Ivan and Tatyana, not an uncommon arrangement for single young people. The family's apartment—centrally located with three bedrooms—is quite large by Russian standards. Grisha is unusual in that he is the only family member who did not go to university. He went straight to work following his graduation from a vocational school.

Grisha believes in God and thinks of himself as a Russian patriot. "You cannot turn Russia into a Western country," he says.

"We are not Westerners and we don't want to be like them. Western virtues are revolting to me," he states categorically.

When I ask him to identify some of these "revolting virtues," he tells me that "to be thrifty, sensible and moderate is not attractive to Russians."

Most of his friends in the factory where he works feel that way too. He thinks that young people who believe that a free market economy will deliver American-like wealth to Russia, are stupid and naive. Communist ideology never appealed to Grisha, yet he misses the basic security and a sense of safety, prestige and unity that he thought were part of the Soviet communist system. He is deeply pessimistic about the future.

Tatyana, his mother, says about her son, "Grisha is a nationalist and, above all, he likes the status quo. I am very worried about him. He is not going to make it in a free market system, because essentially he likes to be taken care of and he avoids responsibility."

Tatyana, who used to be optimistic about the course of change in Russia, is becoming less so as time goes on. She observes that in virtually every family, there is a great polarization of views, opinions and values, her family being a vivid example. Tatyana believes that her other son, Ilya, will thrive in the new environment. As for her and her husband, she feels they will grudgingly adapt.

"Before, under communism, we all knew our place. Sure there was hypocrisy and lies, but we knew how to see right through it all. Today, only a very few people know their place with any real clarity. Ilya is one of them. Capitalism works for him. Ilya believes in working hard, taking risks and responsibility, and receiving material rewards in return."

Tatyana described some of the paradoxes of present-day Russian reality that influence people's sense of values.

"Pensioners," she says, "have no money but they have apartments, often quite large and luxurious by Russian standards. They don't usually need that much space; yet, since they still pay little for it and the apartment is the only thing they have, they tenaciously hold on to it. Sometimes pensioners become the objects of hostility from young people, who not only don't have apartments, but cannot even realistically hope to have one any time soon. Apartments are expensive and scarce. So the elderly are frequently preyed upon by those who want to come into possession of their precious homes."

There is a growing rift between young and old resulting from this housing situation. But while young people don't have apartments, they often have opportunities that the elderly could not even dream of. It is no secret that the new private enterprises and joint ventures, can and do demand, "young employees only." Age discrimination is widely practiced in Russia and there is no protection against it.

"The principles of communism were not so bad," says Tatyana. "My parents believed that while they may not have been able to see a better future, their children and grandchildren definitely would. That influenced their entire attitude to life. There was to be a better tomorrow and this faith made sacrifices and hardship easier to take."

Tatyana finds it difficult, if not impossible, to believe in a sunny future for her children and grandchildren. Instead, she sees a decline of community values.

The things most Russians complain about, such as consumerism, a preoccupation with money and material things, greed and selfishness, competition and individualism, are features of capitalism. But features like hard work, a sense of responsibility, thriftiness, tolerance for others, and respect for achievement, which are found in capitalism as well, are not greatly appreciated either.

"The West will never succeed in remaking Russia into its own image. We are not a nation of shopkeepers and accountants," Tatyana states emphatically.

Tatyana is very worried about the present generation of teenagers.

"They, more than any other age group, are torn between the past and the future. They don't believe in anything. They are tragic."

Tatyana is in a characteristically fatalistic Russian mood.

"That's us, the Russians. We might be attracted to your values for a while, but, sooner or later, we say 'to hell with it.'"

Her husband, Ivan, does not offer any personal views about values because, in his words, "I study values for a living."

Ilya disagrees with his mother, father and older brother.

"Capitalism and the free market, and all the values that are part of this package, are fine with me."

The only view that Ilya shares with his family is his firm belief that, above all, "Russia needs law and order" to allow capitalism and its values "to take root, to grow and to bloom."

The Four of Us Against the World

I MET ALINA through mutual friends and she invited me into her spacious three-room apartment. In her forties, she is a manager of a joint-venture company. She makes very good money, $500 a month, but has to support her entire family with this.

There is her husband, Vladimir, a fifty-year-old, unemployed toolmaker who drinks because "what else is he to do with himself," as Alina puts it, and who beats her on occasion because "he is a man and he is unhappy and frustrated."

There are two children. Her daughter, Edvokya, twenty, is married to Alex, who "is no good" and who left her after two years of marriage. "So much the better," was Alina's succinct comment.

Her son, twenty-two-year-old Seryozha, studies accounting, like his mother did. Alina has great hopes for him. She thinks he will be able to land a job with her company after he graduates, but in the meantime his school costs money because it is one of the new, private institutes that has mushroomed in Russia in the past three years.

"Our world exists almost exclusively within the walls of our apartment," says Alina.

"Everything else is a hostile environment. It is only our family that matters. It is this small world that we try to protect from the outside world."

And her husband agrees. "That's right, nobody will protect us these days, neither the state nor the police. We have only ourselves and we have to protect ourselves against our own people."

"People don't trust each other now. We are afraid," sums up Alina.

But then she is quick to add that her family is, in some way, more affected and frightened than most because they have been touched by horror very recently.

Only a year earlier, Seryozha's twenty-year-old girlfriend was murdered. She was killed in her family's apartment by thieves who broke in in the middle of the day. Her father walked into the apartment as she was being stabbed, and the intruders turned on him. The neighbours responded to the screams but it was too late to save them. Father and daughter were both killed. One bandit escaped; the other was caught by the neighbours and beaten to death.

"It is the poverty and hardship of everyday life that lead people to such cruelty," says Alina.

Vladimir feels that it is more than that.

"Our country's moral fabric has disintegrated and in its place came American values."

"What do you mean by 'American values'?" I ask Vladimir.

"It is the brutal, mindless force that is being glorified in all the American movies that our children go to see; it is non-stop violence."

He angrily continues.

"Nobody ever grieves or even feels sorry for the life lost. It seems that the more you kill and disfigure without mercy, the more of a hero you become. That's what they feed our young, your movie makers and our movie distributors. Those are the role models for our youth."

I turn to Seryozha and ask him if he and his sister go to many American

This teenager's grandmother told the author she is worried about the girl's
dieting and skinny looks.

movies of the kind his father described.

"You mean they make other kinds of movies too?" Vladimir asks.

"Yes, of course," says Seryozha. "My friends and I go to see all the American movies that are shown in Moscow."

"Why?" I want to know.

"Because," says Seryozha, "they are different and exciting and, naturally, we all want to see Rambo and the other characters doing everything they want to and getting away with it too."

Seryozha pauses, and just when I thought he wasn't going to say any more, he adds, "I changed. Ever since Liza got killed. I changed."

Liza was Seryozha's first love and he was profoundly affected by her death. In two days, the family was going to the cemetery to mark the first anniversary of Liza's death.

Alina says that all parents are afraid for their children, especially for teenagers, and try to figure out ways to keep them off the streets, which is virtually impossible, or to get them out of the country, which is not easy either.

Edvokya wasn't home yet, and since it was dark, I asked if she was expected home soon. Uneasy silence followed my question.

"We don't know when she will be back. She doesn't tell us," said Vladimir sounding angry again. Silence again until Alina spoke.

"Our daughter keeps bad company. Ever since her husband left, she runs around with a bunch of good-for-nothing characters."

I didn't press the issue. Vladimir pushed his chair back, got up and walked out of the kitchen. Alina looked after him and then turned to me.

"He has gone to drink again. He drinks because he has no job. He drinks because our Edvokya went bad. He drinks because he cannot do anything about it and he doesn't feel like a man any more."

Then she tells me that Edvokya always was a problem. Three years earlier, while still in high school, she became pregnant. Luckily, the boy married her. The baby was born dead. The marriage fell apart and Edvokya began to drink. Alina suspects she might be taking drugs and prostituting herself as well.

"When she comes home, which is not often, she wears clothes that cost hundreds of dollars, and she does not take much money from me. She won't talk to me either, she just stares at me and says, 'Mama, all I want is to rest and feel safe for a few days,' and then she disappears again. What are we to do? Her father wanted to kill her at first. Now, he just cries and drinks and beats me from time to time."

I look at Edvokya's framed picture on top of the television. A lovely young woman, her picture stands next to that of Liza.

I asked Alina and Seryozha whether they believe in God. Alina told me she believes very deeply and that it is religion that makes it possible for her to cope with life.

"I go to church every Sunday. I rest there. My mother always was a believer. Of course, under communism we didn't go to church but my grandmother told me once: 'Don't reject God. Life will show whether you believe in him or not. God will come to you when you are ready for him.' And she was right. It wasn't till I turned forty, but I found God and that helps me get through life."

Alina said that she doesn't see too many teenagers and young people in church but many children are brought by their parents and grandparents.

Seryozha agrees. "I believe in something," he said, "but I don't like the clergy and churches."

"Why not?" I asked.

"Because," said Seryozha, "in church, they say mass and it is so stupid, repetitious and mindless. That's what turns off any thinking person. All my friends feel that way."

"But I find it restful. For me the repetition brings comfort," says Alina, "but I must agree with Seryozha that our church ritual does turn off the intelligentsia. You know, our great symbolist poet, Blok, once said that 'the Russian intelligentsia believes in God but does not go to Church. They believe in ideas but they don't like to practice them.'"

I asked Seryozha whether he likes to read and whether Russian literature means much to him. "Not much," he said, and added that most young people don't care for books either. They prefer television, videos, and movies.

At this point Vladimir joins us again. It's obvious that he has been drinking, and he immediately dominates the conversation.

"God? You ask about God? Yes, I believe in God, but I don't understand him. But you know what I think? Maybe Dostoievsky was right. Remember what he said? 'If there is no God, everything is permitted.' Maybe there isn't any God and that's why we are surrounded by all this evil and filth and degradation."

Alina was trying to interrupt him, but to no avail. I stayed a while longer, but it became increasingly clear that Vladimir's mood was becoming very gloomy and he was starting to repeat himself. I decided to leave.

"At times like this," Alina said, walking me to the door, "one must let him drink himself to sleep and hope that he will do just that. If I am lucky, it will be soon; if not, he may hit me once or twice. But he is a good man and he never hits me very hard. You see, he is so unhappy and it is his soul that is hurting. Vodka is his only escape. And believe me, he is very sorry every time it happens. He is decent; he only drinks at home and he is true to me."

A Good Profession

I MET SERGEI ON A BUS in Moscow in the middle of the day. At that hour the bus was nearly empty. The driver had run out of tickets—a frequent enough occurrence—and Sergei generously offered me one. Over the course of our long ride we talked.

Sergei is a bookkeeper, a good profession to have in the new Russia. He was between jobs. He left a position with a state enterprise and was about to start working for a private company for five times the amount of money—a most enviable position to be in anywhere. Sergei felt rather pleased with life but was also quite aware that luck can change.

"Before," he said, "we had security; today, we have opportunity, or at least some of us do."

Despite his own personal good luck, Sergei saw himself and his forty-plus generation as a deformed generation. "We are like robots. We stopped fighting and only few of us are capable of independent thinking.

"Mind you," he said, "my profession was never considered very glamorous by my friends. In fact, many considered me downright boring. I wasn't what they thought of as being 'creative' or 'imaginative' and yet, today my artistic and creative friends are jobless, or barely making ends meet, while I am doing better than ever. For them, that's just proof that capitalism is not suited to free-spirited characters with 'Russian souls' like themselves, but only to the boring ones like me."

Sergei laughs but I have an odd feeling that he is not altogether convinced that his "creative" friends are wrong. Sergei has two sons, aged twenty-three and fifteen. He thinks there is a world of difference between these two age groups.

He is very worried and concerned about his younger son. "Nothing matters to him except money and material possessions."

His older son, who studies business and accounting, is fluent in English and is "a decent and responsible human being."

Sergei doesn't feel that today's Russian youth is particularly cynical or corrupted. But, while young people in their early twenties are chiefly concerned with practical questions of adapting and surviving, teenagers are dangerously influenced by the sensationalist Russian and foreign media that focus on extremes. Neither age group, Sergei feels, is interested in politics or politicians.

When I asked Sergei whether he or his family were religious, he told me that the whole family consider themselves to be atheists. But he offered the opinion that it is mostly the children of very well-off parents who turn to various forms of religion.

"They don't need to worry about money and survival, so they are attracted to both the Russian Orthodox faith and other religious groups and movements."

Sergei thinks that only a small fraction of youth gets involved with religion. However, he observed that many older people turn to church for guidance and direction.

"Before, there was a state religion, communism, with its own symbols, rituals and clearly-defined values. Now it is gone and everything seems to be permitted. People are lost. They want some sense of order, whether it comes from the state or God as they understand it."

When I Grow Up I Will Go With Foreigners

I SPOKE with fourteen-year-old Darya in rather unusual circumstances. Darya was begging on the street in the vicinity of the Intourist Hotel in the centre of Moscow. I was struck by this pretty girl, dressed in jeans and a T-shirt, asking passers-by, in English, for spare change!

She turned out to be a Russian high school student from an ordinary family; she "specialized" in getting money from English-speaking foreigners. I gave her a dollar and she agreed to talk to me.

She explained how careful she must be to keep her distance from the prostitutes and their pimps.

55

To get married and live happily ever after is still what most
young Russian women want.

"They could beat me up," she said.

Darya started her "job" two months earlier. She spends two hours a day, five days a week, at her spot. She clears about twenty dollars a week. It is more than her mother makes as a full-time clerk in a state enterprise. Darya has a six-year-old sister. Her mother is divorced and her father's whereabouts are unknown. Darya earns more than half of the family's income by begging in English.

Darya has protection. She pays two dollars a week to a boy who is sixteen and who looks out for her. When she gets older, she will "go with foreigners" to make really good money. Darya's chief qualification for her begging job is her remarkable knowledge of English.

Darya says that she really doesn't understand what things like democracy or free market mean and she is not interested in politics.

She likes all the "wonderful things in stores" and thinks it is good that they are there, but she doesn't believe that she will be able to buy such things until she begins going with foreigners. She seems to be fatalistically resigned that this will happen sometime within the next two years when she graduates from high school. Darya does not plan to go to college.

"Maybe I will meet someone rich and marry him," she says. "Then I could help my family, have nice things for myself, and be able to travel as well."

Darya talks and sounds like any teenage girl. She tells me about her school.

"We study a lot about the past, you know, before the Revolution and Lenin. Everything was good then when we had czars," she says.

When I ask her whether she likes school, she tells me that she feels sorry for her teachers. "Why?" I ask in surprise.

"Because" says Darya, "kids don't respect them. The students behave really badly. They walk out of the class in the middle of a lecture. They curse teachers to their faces, especially the women teachers, and they just don't care. Once, the students even pushed one teacher down the stairs because she told them she wouldn't tolerate their behavior in the classroom."

Shocked, I asked what happened then.

"Nothing," says Darya. "What are they going to do? Nobody is afraid any more—except the teachers, of course."

Darya also tells me that most of her girlfriends want to be models, movie stars, or prostitutes for foreigners. Boys dream of making lots of money, driving fast American cars and owning guns. Both boys and girls think that their parents and teachers, who work hard and make little money, are fools and failures. Consequently, young people avoid living lives similar to those of the adults around them.

Darya's grandmother, who lived with the family (and who died two years ago), told Darya about God.

"God," says Darya, "is something that is higher than man." But Darya doesn't go to church and she does not think of herself as a religious person.

"Some of my friends, not many, attend church from time to time because it is fashionable now. They go a couple of times and then they stop because they get bored."

When I ask Darya what she thinks is the most important thing in life, she tells me without a moment's hesitation, "family." After "going with foreigners" she wants to marry, preferably a rich man, and have a family because "to have babies and to care for them is the most important thing in life if you are a woman."

Of God and Healers

I MET BRIEFLY with Igor who is president of an organization that calls itself Young People for God and Motherland. He is in his mid-twenties and he claims that his group has a hundred thousand members across Russia.

"If there is no religion, there is no spirit," he tells me.

Igor claims that he and his followers are not interested or involved in politics, nor do they relate to the official structures of the Russian Orthodox Church.

"God has to be restored and cultivated in people's souls or there will be total anarchy, chaos and spiritlessness."

Igor and his followers believe that the way to restore God is "to restore the spiritual Russian values of the past, such as humility, patience and endurance."

None of the young people that I spoke with, in groups or individually, were familiar with Igor's movement, but his sentiments and convictions about the need for restoration of "traditional spiritual Russian values" were quite popular.

Virtually all of the fifteen young female students from Moscow University, with whom I talked about their lives, claimed to believe in God. However, nearly all of them rejected the Russian Orthodox Church or any other formal religious structure as a means of expressing their religious beliefs.

Yet most of the girls were baptized recently. In many cases, it was the mother or grandmother or some other female member of the family who initiated the process. Very few of these young women go to church. They told me that many of their friends, including some males, embraced religion in their teens but, like them, shun the church itself.

"For me, religion means history, culture and heritage," says Katya.

"To me it means spirituality," exclaims Lyuba.

"Religion is all that is the best inside me," announces Masha.

Then, as often was the case in my encounters with this group, the girls all began to talk at once.

"The church, and all that it represents, is all so naive. It is something for peasants but ... I believe in God."

"There must be something beyond man; the universe must be bigger than man."

"We all believe in God. It is our family tradition."

"The Church is not important. It is the inner God that matters."

"Religion is needed. Humanity has to believe in something."

"God and spirituality belong in the human soul, not in church. Men and women do not need a middle man to communicate with God. All these mumbo-jumbo prayers, that's a joke. They don't mean anything, they don't express anything. Why say them? It's a waste of time! As a ritual, a theatre, the church is nice once in a long while, but nothing else. Yet I consider myself a deeply religious person," says Lyuba.

Vera is the only one in the group who has radically different views.

"No, I don't believe in God," she says. "It is all fairy tales to me. It was invented to have control over people. To keep people in line. I certainly am not a communist but I agree with Marx who said that 'religion is the opium of the people.'"

Katya interrupts Vera.

"What about the line from Dostoievsky—'If there is no God, everything is permitted.' How do you respond to that?"

Vera is untroubled.

"There is another line, I don't remember whose: 'If there was no God, man would invent him.'" And she continues, "Man needs God as a narcotic—

With their shaved heads and orange robes, followers of the International
Society for Krishna Consciousness, can be seen and heard chanting
"Hare Krishna," in virtually every part of Russia.

numbing the pain, imagining rewards, or as a whip. To the simple folk, religion gives hope and promise."

Mariya who was silent up to this point, joins in.

"It is a Russian tradition that power comes from God, and to this end, religion was always used in Russia as a tool of power. But, I think religion and spirituality do not have to overlap and I sense a great spiritual need."

Nearly every time I had a conversation with a Russian over the past three years, no matter what we were discussing, sooner or later, the subject of faith healing would come up. I didn't take it very seriously at first, but on my trip in the summer of 1994, I decided that the phenomenon of faith healing was too large to be ignored.

Valentina, a fifty-seven-year-old retired cook, told me that she lost fifty pounds of excess weight by drinking water "tele-charged" by a popular healer. I laughed at her story then, but I was to hear so many versions of the same story from so many other Russians, that I began to listen more carefully.

Faith healing, parapsychology, auto-suggestion and white magic, started becoming popular in the former Soviet Union in the mid-1980s, the early days of Gorbachev's *perestroika*. By the end of the decade, a number of television programs featured various healers. The two most popular ones were, and still are, a former journalist-turned-healer, Allan Chumak, and psychologist and hypnotist Anatoly Kashpirovsky. Even though their shows are no longer aired in Russia because they were accused of "using their hypnotic abilities to influence political judgment," their popularity is immense. Not only are these men fanatically revered in Russia, but their "tele-magic" is now broadcast to large audiences all over Eastern Europe.

Russia was always susceptible to a spiritual approach to life's problems. Rasputin, the most famous Russian healer, was a friend of Czarina Alexandra and a power behind the throne of Nicholas II (the last czar of Russia). He was one of many Russians who claimed to have special powers because he was in touch with another world and another kind of energy.

Hundreds of thousands of Russian men and women, most of them middle-aged and older, are the most ardent believers in the powers of these healers.

"Say what you want," my last year's hostess told me, "Chumak and Kashpirovsky do cure people." Vera is a fifty-six-year-old woman with a university education and she swears that watching Kashpirovsky's programs cured her kidney disease.

Virtually every person I spoke with this year told me stories of miraculous cures for diabetes, tumors, paralysis, depression, allergies and countless other ills. New Age healers appear to be taking care of what the disintegrating Russian health care system is not able to handle.

Now that Chumak and Kashpirovsky's faith healing shows are no longer on live television, Russians are buying videotapes of the old shows. And they claim they are just as effective. I watched a video of Chumak in action. He stares, waves his hands, and doesn't say much. Apparently, the people who are at home watching him, place bottles of water and jars containing creams in front of the screen and believe that the water and creams assume healing properties through "tele-charged energies" sent by Chumak; drinking the water and rubbing the creams on affected parts of the body will heal their assorted illnesses.

I haven't met a single Russian who would dismiss the healers' movement or mock it. The movement is taken very seriously. The very prestigious Russian Academy of Science has established a special commission to investigate the "auras" of healers. While the commission has not yet arrived at specific conclusions or recommendations, it has indicated that "research into the matter has colossal possibilities."

Anatoly Kashpirovsky demonstrated on television how, through the power of suggestion, he anaesthetized a woman (who could not tolerate normal anesthesia) during abdominal surgery. As with Chumak, hundreds of thousands of Russians and East Europeans claim to be healed by Kashpirovsky.

According to reports in the Russian media, Kashpirovsky was formally accused by politicians and doctors of "manipulating the human brain to influence politics." He is said to be responsible for Zhirinovsky's 24 percent showing in the December 1993 parliamentary elections. Subsequently, Kashpirovsky was declared dangerous by Yeltsin's government and barred from Russian television. This didn't stop Kashpirovsky from running for the Duma himself and getting elected as a deputy on Zhirinovsky's ticket.

I was told that many Russian intellectuals travel to remote Russian villages, in an attempt to find old people who know "the old ways of healing." University professors I talked with about Russian politics told me very seriously that the healers' movement is a positive development.

"Nothing in Russia now seems to be under control. People are disillusioned with politics and the economy and they are trying somehow to deal with their personal lives. More and more, people believe that the only way to change the quality of their lives is to change their consciousness. Religion, parapsychology, yoga, faith healing, hypnosis, and white magic are taking hold of people's minds. I believe it is preferable to alcoholism, violence or the worship of things and money," said Stephan, a forty-two-year-old psychologist from Moscow University.

The Russian Soul

A GROUP OF TEN YOUNG MALE STUDENTS I talked with had the same strong feelings about the need to believe in something, as did the female students I had interviewed.

"One has to live up to one's beliefs."

"You have to strive in life for something higher. Man has to have ideals, otherwise life is not worth living."

"You must live in accord with yourself."

"A person has to live for others, otherwise life has no meaning. One has to give of oneself."

"The family is the most important part of life."

There was consensus among the students that if there is to be a future for Russia, there must be a revival of spiritual or religious values. The phrase repeated most often was that there "cannot be a Russia without Russian soul."

Everyone had a lot to say when I pressed for elaboration on the mystical "Russian soul."

"You see," said Igor, "Yeltsin, in people's eyes, represents the Russian soul and Gorbachev does not. Gorbachev, with all his intellect and ideas, does not belong to Russia and the Russian tradition. The population instinctively felt this and that's why they disowned him. Yeltsin, however, though not as intelligent or knowledgeable, is all Russian, and people respond to this. His drinking, womanizing, fits of depression and periods of inaction, endear him to us. It is his Russian soul that they recognize. By your standards, his treatment of the Duma in October 1993 was barbaric, but it was a truly Russian way of doing things. Yeltsin is like a Russian peasant; he knows when to use force and when to be brutal. He gets respect."

Heads around the room nodded in agreement.

"Mind you," said Kiril, "we are not talking about politics or ideas *per se*; we are talking about the spirit of things."

When I asked how they would rate Zhirinovsky in this area, they told me that, even though he expresses ideas close to many Russians, he does not represent the Russian soul the way Yeltsin does. Apparently, to manifest the Russian soul one has to be earnest and gloomy with a touch of tragedy. Zhirinovsky's clowning disqualifies him.

And when I asked what they perceived as the greatest threat to the Russian soul, they told me that the Americanization and commercialization of Russian society represent real danger. These students argued that Western values are essentially alien to the majority of Russians.

"Russians are not a nation of slaves but they like to be ruled and taken care of by the state," said Fedya.

"That's the Russian mentality or the Russian soul, so to speak. We have it in our blood. We have been conditioned to be that way for hundreds of years. That's why communism wasn't an assault upon our people; it was simply a continuation of what we knew before," he concluded.

"Right," interjected Kiril. "That's why we want the president to play the role of czar; that's why your parliamentary democracy is essentially foreign to us. That's why so many of us applauded Yeltsin when he bombed Parliament."

"America cannot understand Russia; we speak different languages," said Ivan, who was quiet until then. "We don't need American dollars either. Our rich people are richer than anybody elsewhere. We love excess."

I tried to point out that everything I was hearing seemed to contradict my observations that young people in Russia love everything American, and American dollars in particular. I suggested that maybe the young Russians are worshipping a new God—money, rather than the spirit. I asked this group why they sounded so different from their peers.

I got a passionate response.

"You see," one said, "that proves that you think like an American and really do not understand us, because, in fact, we are not different from the other young people at all. But yes, we are different from Americans and other Westerners."

They said that while young Americans and Westerners want to save some of the money they make and to spend some of it, young Russians want to have it and spend it all!

"Russians are not stupid!" exclaimed Igor. "They don't want to work to make money; they want to have it without working!"

"Yes!" said Fedya, "in Russia we work to make money so we can spend it on vodka; invite friends; be merry; waste it all; be sorry; feel guilty; repent, and then start all over again. To sin and to repent... that's our Russian soul. The West does not understand this. To be thrifty and moderate and neat and orderly and responsible and good—these virtues are not attractive to us."

"You in the West admire characters who have a clear sense of purpose, who don't stray from the chosen path and who, through the sheer power of will and strength of their determination, succeed," Andrei told me.

"We in Russia are more impressed with the ability to endure, to sacrifice, to suffer, and to feel compassionate. These are traditional Russian Orthodox values."

I wanted to know what these values can possibly mean to drunk teenagers I saw on Russian streets.

Igor explained.

"Let's say a group of teenagers notices a dirty, homeless bum lying on the street. He smells, he is covered with sores, and he is drunk and disheveled. Our teenagers might easily walk up to him, give him money, a shirt of their own, some vodka, kiss him, and then walk away. They are likely to feel a certain affection for him rather than revulsion. They would never harm him even though they might rough up a decent looking passer-by just for fun. Russians 'feel' for the 'low' ones. The same group may rape a lone girl, just for fun, but they won't touch an old beggar woman sleeping on the street. That's their sense of right and wrong."

I found the difference in attitudes between male and female students astonishing. Girls, while emphatically concerned with spiritual values, interpreted them quite differently than male students. Absent were mystical references to the Russian soul. In fact, the young women were inclined to disassociate themselves from the distinctive values claimed by the males.

"I think we should forget our Russian character, whatever it is supposed to mean, and think globally. I believe in humanity, and the sooner we forget our so-called Russian soul, the better," said Mariya emphatically.

Masha supported her.

"Yes, we are all people and we are more alike than we are different. It is the politicians who try to exploit our feelings of insecurity and push us to rally under the banners of nationalism and these so-called national differences. As far as I am concerned, women everywhere care the same way for their children and their families. The rest is entirely secondary."

"I would be the happy if there were no borders anywhere to fight for or to die defending. I believe in brotherhood," Katya said with passion as the other girls nodded in agreement.

When I asked them if they would leave Russia to live somewhere else, nearly all of them told me that while they would love to travel outside Russia, they think of Russia as home. Some added, however, that many young people are quite ready to leave even though it is believed that outside Russia, Russians are known to feel like second-class citizens.

My old friend Leonid, the film director, whose opinions I value highly, when asked whether he thought there was such a thing as a Russian soul, didn't hesitate for a moment.

"If there is a relationship between having a soul and the capacity for suffering, then, yes, we Russians do have a very special soul, indeed! Nobody can suffer as much as Russians and nobody can endure as much. If the sheer volume of, and capacity for, suffering makes Russians more soulful than anybody else, then yes, we do have a collective Russian soul."

Then he asked me. "Do you know the difference between an optimist and a pessimist?"

Before I could answer he said, "They have different dates for the end of the world."

For Russians, Leonid feels, the world ends or nearly ends many times over. The Russian people are perennial pessimists and they always expect the worst. Not only that, they collectively believe that "the worse things get, the better," because "once your world ends, you can begin to build a new one."

Leonid thinks that Russian history determined this type of attitude and that extremism has always fared better with Russians than common sense and moderation.

"No reforms and improvements for us. We go for a cataclysm and a total turnover. Then, if it does not work, because it can't, we suffer, we accuse each other and endure until the next crash, whether we call it a revolution or radical reforms."

Leonid also believes that Russians don't really enjoy working. "We don't have a work ethic. The process of working does not interest us very much. Our goal is not to work but to be done with whatever we are doing as quickly as possible. It doesn't matter whether it is done well or not. The important thing is to finish doing it and be free. That's our concept of freedom: not working."

I wondered whether this lack of passion for work was a feature developed under communism and Leonid vehemently restated his original point.

"No. Russians never cared for work. They don't want to be bothered. They don't care if they make a lot of money either. As long as they have some minimum that is regular and safe, they are content. And that is what they would rather have. A Russian would rather steal than earn. That's the Russian soul for you."

I found what Leonid was saying very distressing, and suggested to him that such generalizations are dangerous. He responded by advising me to familiarize myself with Russian literature.

"Why do you think our great writers were concerned with the Russian soul? Precisely because we are so flawed. We are capable of great extremes, we can be sinners, we can be saints, but we don't know how to be 'normal' the way you in the West are."

He continued, "A typical Russian does not place value on human life, his own or others. That's a very Russian characteristic. A man who drinks destroys himself. The Russian way of drinking destroys a man quickly and mercilessly. He is a slave to it and he knows it. He detests himself, so he drinks more to forget. Drinking and self-loathing become the most important features of Russian lives. One perpetuates the other. But drinking also gives one moments of glory. That's when one feels his 'soul.' Some believe that these are the moments in life worth living for."

Oddly enough, even though more and more Russian women deal with the misery of their lives by drinking, their drinking is never perceived as 'spiritual,' the way a man's drinking is often described.

I asked Leonid whether he truly believed what he was telling me, or whether he was simply repeating clichés that always seem to surface when talking about Russians. He was serious.

"Maybe the majority of my countrymen would not use the terms I have used, but you will find that it is what they think and feel. Some could tell you that they drink today to escape their sense of impotency; some drink to escape their families and women, but they all run away from themselves."

"Why would a Russian's drinking be that different from anyone else's?" I asked.

"Because of our Russian soul," answered Leonid. "On one hand, we have this overflowing spirituality; on the other, we have this stupor-like inability to act, this paralysis of will, a fatalistic tendency to self-analyze, to self-accuse and to self-immolate emotionally. We seem to be set on destroying ourselves and others. We suffer while we do it but we wouldn't have it any other way.

"Russians are capable of being bestial as a crowd but also warm and generous to a fault. We are a very extreme people. It is because of our dark Russian souls," Leonid summed up.

This last statement is dismissed by Bulat, a businessman who has provided me with interesting insights on a variety of subjects over the years.

"All that nonsense about the Russian soul is just that. It is a literary creation that has no relation to reality. You can say the same things about any nation. All these national stereotypes!"

I asked him then whether he believed in God.

"I am not practicing any religion but I am kind of religious. It is something new, my own personal development. I don't think of it as a result of new religious freedoms because I don't go to churches and I don't care for the clergy. I never will. For me, religion is something you carry inside you. It is a sense of being linked to the Universe and I don't think that my link is any different because I have a Russian soul. I don't buy that."

How To Be Happy

VALERY, A SOCIOLOGIST, has a radio program called "How to Be Happy." Upon learning about my book, he allowed me to listen to some of the tapes of his show.

The program goes on the air live every day at five p.m. Listeners call Valery to express their feelings, to explain why they are happy or unhappy. Usually more than one person is on the line at the same time—sometimes a couple, a family, or a group of friends. They laugh, cry, fight, and make up on the air. When they call Valery, they expect him to tell them what to do: how they can become happy. On one of the tapes I listened to, Valery talked about the simple, universal joys of life for about ten minutes. He spoke of the seasons, the leaves turning color, about loving somebody—a man, a woman, a child—and he spoke of giving and receiving, and about being kind in a small way at least once a day.

"How to Be Happy" has been on the air for just over a year. At the beginning, Valery told me, people were quite upset with the show. They seemed outraged that someone would talk about such things while the world around them was drowning in misery. "Life is impossible now, how can you talk about happiness?" Valery told them that everybody has at least a few good moments here and there amidst all the unhappiness. Sharing these moments with others, Valery told his listeners, will give them pleasure.

The show has become very popular. People of all ages call in about everything under the sun. Often a caller gives advice to another caller, and, while about two-thirds of the callers are older people, some topics attract a young audience as well.

One time Valery asked his listeners what kind of state they prefer to live in—paternal or maternal? The Russian understanding of the paternal state is one that leaves you alone. A maternal state takes care of you. Teenage callers to the show all expressed a preference for a paternal state. In their eyes, the United States personified such a state. The older callers more predictably expressed the sentiment that they would be happier in a maternal state, and many named Canada as their choice.

Another time, Valery was discussing consumerism and asked his audience whether they thought of shopping as a happy time. While many callers said that they enjoyed buying things very much, they stressed that it is not so much the activity of shopping that makes them happy but rather being able to get things they need and like. Russians rarely had the opportunity to do so in the past. Shopping in itself is not seen as a recreational activity as it is in the West. It is the result of shopping that gives pleasure to Russians—to share the purchased goods with friends and family; to impress them; to better one's life with the purchase. Russians buy things and treasure them. However, shopping is still perceived as necessary drudgery.

A number of callers observed that a dramatic shift has occurred in Russian

Twenty or even ten years ago, Russians would deny themselves many things in order to buy books, particularly books that were banned or censored and could only be bought on the black market. At one time, Solzhenitsyn's books were in great demand. They were copied and shared with friends. Since photocopying was not accessible in the Soviet Union, books, most often published abroad or underground, were copied on a typewriter with carbon paper. To search out and buy such a book, to read it, to share it with friends and to discuss it afterwards, was considered one of life's great pleasures—albeit an expensive one.

In 1985, more and more books became available and today almost any title can be easily purchased in Russia. The problem is that people no longer buy or read them. According to Valery, callers no longer mention the importance of books and the pleasure derived from literature. They rarely refer to literary characters or to writers as their models or heroes, as was the case in the past.

The market is flooded with European and American mass literature: thrillers and romances. One no longer sees cab drivers reading Dostoievsky or Tolstoy; instead, these authors have been replaced by the daily sensationalist press. While members of the older generation still perceive themselves as intellectuals, their children seem to have abandoned literature.

When Valery asked listeners to call in and tell him what they thought about Solzhenitsyn's return to Russia after twenty years of exile in the United States, most of the callers viewed Solzhenitsyn as a stranger to both the new Russia and to capitalism. They perceived him as somebody who emerged from the past (the 1960s), and who wanted to revive czarist Russia. While the older callers at least knew who Solzhenitsyn was, younger Russians didn't know and didn't care.

One of the show's young callers told the host that "these days even if Christ himself was to show up in Russia, nobody would notice because people are so tired and busy just surviving." Valery asked the young caller what he does in place of reading for pleasure and was told that "fun means being entertained, best of all by an American action movie like *Rambo*."

On another show Valery asked the younger callers to talk about their parents.

"Are your parents happy or not?" he asked. In an overwhelming response, teenagers called in to say that their parents were quite unhappy.

"My parents are very bitter."

"Mine are disappointed with everything that is happening."

"My mother and father are very pessimistic and think their lives are over. They also fight constantly about everything."

"My parents are really worried about the future and about me and my sister."

"Since father left us, my mother is afraid of everything."

"My parents feel that since 1991, their lives went down the drain."

There was only one caller who had something different to say.

"My parents are so busy making money that they don't have time to worry about happiness. I really cannot tell if they are happy or not. But I guess I liked it better when we had less money and more time together."

The Russian Character

"How to Be Happy" radio host Valery had some observations and opinions about Russians and what he called the Russian character. We talked about the apparent failure of the economic reforms or "shock treatment" which began in January 1992, and about the problems reformers are experiencing in Russia.

"Reforms should start with the understanding of the nation's character. Russia's unique character and the fact that Russia is very different from Western countries were never really taken into consideration when introducing reforms," he continued.

"In fact," he elaborated, "the reformers made the elementary mistake of deciding that the Russian character does not exist, that it is nothing but a false stereotype."

"What is this Russian character if not a stereotype?" I asked.

"The major characteristic of the Russian people is their amazing credulity," said Valery.

"Russians simply don't know how not to trust. For Russians, to believe means to be alive."

I expressed some doubt about these trusting Russians and Valery explained that he is talking about the Russians collectively.

"As a group, Russians are motivated not by reason, calculation, or a desire for comfort; they are always motivated by beliefs such as there is right and wrong, good and evil, and one has to make a choice."

"How does this relate to reforms or reformers?" I asked.

"You see," continued Valery, "Russians accepted *perestroika* and *glasnost;* and then accepted the reforms and reformers, not as a result of a rational choice or a practical concern, but simply as a result of believing the political leaders of the moment. Few Russians really understood the changes that were to take place but many had faith. We Russians love to believe in miracles."

Valery told me time and time again how the people calling him on his show would express the faith that maybe, maybe this time, something will work; why not give it a try. As living conditions deteriorated, the population seemed even more keen on believing.

"But they all complain," I pointed out.

"Yes," he agreed, "but nevertheless, Russians are very patient people. They can endure more than almost anybody and that's another specific Russian characteristic."

Valery believes that because Russians are so capable of enduring hardship, there is no real danger of a social explosion in Russia.

"As long as there is a shadow of faith that maybe another leader or another program will make things better, people will suffer and endure still more," he said.

"But," he cautioned, "the Russian, be it the individual or society as a whole, should not be pushed to the limits—once Russians lose hope and faith, that's the end of the endurance. If Russians get angry, there is no stopping them; they become very dangerous."

I felt that what Valery was telling me reinforced stereotypes the West has about Russia and I questioned their validity. But Valery suggested that these stereotypes are rooted in Russian political culture, traditions, philosophy, and literature. He pointed out that for Russians, both ethics and ideologies are valued, if not more then certainly no less than material welfare.

"It is for ideas and beliefs that Russians will die most readily," he said. He felt that history vividly illustrated this point.

I questioned how easy would it be for Russians to switch from a communist to a capitalist mentality and value system. Valery felt that while it may seem easy on the surface, because, after all, everybody wants to have things, it is going to be much more difficult on a deeper, psychological level to make the transition.

Western candy machines, built like Fort Knox, are appearing on the streets of Moscow, St. Petersburg and other Russian cities. Popular with Russian youth, the candies are sold at Western prices.

"Russians are maximalists and nihilists at heart," he said. "As a rule, they tend toward extreme measures and extreme means. They like to take care of all the social problems once and for all."

"You see," said Valery, "Russians like to make radical changes, not just gradual adjustments; they would prefer to destroy and build anew than to reconstruct. That's why the whole concept of *perestroika*—reconstruction—didn't work with most Russians right from the start. Russians always go for the absolute."

Valery thought that Russians are attracted to extremes because they lack a stable spiritual core.

"A total absence of a real conservatism is the Russians' fatal flaw. Russia achieved the Revolution but never stopped living by the laws of the Revolution. First it was a march toward military communism; then it was the New Economic Policy; then forced collectivization, industrialization and militarization; the rebuilding of communism after World War II; the acceleration, and then the Soviet Union falls apart. The final step was the push toward the free market economy; a push rather than a movement toward it.

"Another Russian characteristic," continued Valery, "is to set grandiose, unrealistic goals. Russians have always done this. The utopian ideals of one set of leaders are replaced with the illusionary ideals of some other leader. Vitality is dissipated, energy is wasted, generations are lost and the end result is minimal or the opposite of what was intended. After each episode, Russia breaks down a bit more and moves backwards. That's why Russia is lagging behind. We Russians always end up in some temporary stage, in the waiting room of history."

It is Valery's opinion that Russians are incapable of making use of Western expertise.

"Practical foreigners give us advice. They tell us: set modest goals and, step by step, try to achieve them. We won't listen. We don't know how to take small steps or to be practical because we want to be the most advanced, the most just, the most spiritual society. We aim for God's kingdom on earth!"

"Aren't you exaggerating just a bit, Valery?" I asked.

"Not at all!" exclaimed Valery. "First, Russian radicals were ready to destroy Russia to achieve their utopian society. Communists, their spiritual heirs, also believed in their vision of the working man's paradise, convinced that all means were justified in obtaining this goal. And don't today's radical reformers also

74

act as if they have a holy mission at stake? Don't they seem to solemnly believe that the speed, the cruelty of the reforms, and the risks taken with society are all justified, because the leading principle is that the faster we race through these difficult changes, the sooner our lives become free and rich?"

Valery concluded our discussion of the Russian character by telling me that Russians are so eager for ideals in which to believe, so anxious to live "not by bread alone," so intent upon maintaining their "unique Russian spirit and character," that they will invent a struggle even if one does not exist. And thus, the Russian people will keep on struggling as long as they believe that the struggle will lead to a "better, more just life."

Zakhar is a driver for the Russian film corporation, Mosfilm. (The name "Mosfilm" is as familiar to Russians as Hollywood is to the rest of the world.) Zakhar is fifty but looks much older—he has no teeth, he is wrinkled, stooped, thin, and shabbily dressed. Though Zakhar received only a fifth-grade education, the moment he begins to speak, he radiates a tremendous energy. His Russian is rich and colorful, filled with proverbs and vivid metaphors.

Zakhar chauffeurs my friend Leonid. Leonid asked Zakhar to show me "his" Moscow. Zakhar and I spent half a day driving around Moscow to places that I would probably never get to see on my own. We toured industrial districts—abandoned factories and beer stands surrounded by worn-out men. We toured a Moscow that is rarely visited by tourists, the Moscow that is ugly and scary, depressing and real.

We talked non-stop and my tape recorder, ignored by Zakhar, worked overtime. Zakhar had an opinion as well as a running commentary on just about everything that we saw during our ride. While he did not always answer my questions directly, in his own way, he would respond to every one of them.

"I have a mind of my own," said Zakhar. "It is not important to say who is right and who is wrong for Russia. I don't care whether he is called Gorbachev or Yeltsin or something else. I have my own pocket and I know when it is empty. It is emptier now than it was under the Reds. And even if there is something in my pocket, I still cannot afford to buy anything with it."

As we were driving through the district known as "Zhil's Kingdom"—the working-class district around the Zhil car factory—Zakhar pointed out the disintegrating sidewalks, the vacant shops, the littered alleys, and the gloomy facades of monolithic apartment buildings with crumbling balconies.

"It is very hard," Zakhar was saying, "and for us, the ordinary, older people, it is not getting better. God knows who they are, these guys at the top. Their names change as circumstances change, and each time for the worse. They all promise, and nobody even bothers to figure out what it is that they are promising."

For Zakhar, society's major problems originated with the dissolution of the Soviet Union.

"Our strength and our importance were in our being together. The separation of the republics took away their strength, and ours with it. People are not stupid. They know it. I talk with lots of guys who drive trucks all over the former Soviet Union. They don't like all this talk about independence. The ordinary folk do not care about it, but the leaders do. They want to keep the power to themselves. They don't want to answer to Moscow or anybody. They have all kinds of slogans to get people excited. And some people react, especially the young ones. Fools are always ready to die..."

We passed a cluster of brightly-colored kiosks—metal stands that sell Western candies such as Mars, Snickers, and Milky Way. Zakhar was indignant about the candy bars.

"Look, for the price of one of these, you could buy ten Russian bars. Who benefits from this? Do we need it?"

That remark led to a tirade about foreign influence, visible everywhere in Russia's urban centres.

"All these foreigners and foreign ideas, they are the worst, all these free economies. To my mind, all it means is that now each man has to fend for himself. Everyone tries to get the best of everybody else and the West, especially the Americans, laugh their heads off looking at us now..."

We were passing a group of young soldiers doing some road work.

"Look at our Red Army; they destroyed it, these reformers." Zakhar makes a spitting sound.

"How can it be that a young man doesn't want to serve in the army? Imagine the nerve. I can understand the young man who is afraid during wartime—he's scared of being killed. But now? When a young, healthy boy doesn't want to serve his country and hides from the draft, it's a real shame. I don't know what the world is coming to. This is not right; he is not acting like a man. He doesn't even understand the meaning of the word 'motherland.' He won't be able to defend his country because he is afraid of gunpowder. He is simply a coward. Men need military skills and these skills don't happen by themselves. You need to learn them in the army."

Zakhar is not easily diverted from what he feels this book-writing foreign woman ought to know.

"Tape this," he says, and I do.

"These reformers and democrats make our country defenseless. They tell us to make money, not war, and our young people listen. Except that they are ready to kill each other for money. It is horrible that so many of our young people have this stupid faith in the West and in America. You see, in Russia, in order to live, people have to believe in something. Before, some believed in Lenin, or Stalin, or communism. Now our youth believe in everything American."

There is a saying in Russia: "You believe, you survive." Zakhar quotes it but tells me that this time, this new religion-faith in all things American— will not work.

"We are Russians, not Americans," he says. "Americans won't give anybody anything for free and they want us to become like them. They tell Yeltsin what to do."

That statement enabled me to ask some questions about Yeltsin, and Zakhar surprised me somewhat with his comments.

"Luckily," said Zakhar, "Yeltsin is not so stupid. He keeps his cards close to his chest. These democrats think that he is one of them but he's not ... because he knows better."

"Is he a communist?" I asked.

"No!" responded Zakhar with great conviction. "No, who needs them! But he is a Russian and he won't sell out to Americans."

I asked Zakhar how he felt about the ultra-nationalist Zhirinovsky. Zakhar said that Zhirinovsky did not appeal to him because he's too much of a clown and "a leader should not let people laugh at him." But he felt that Zhirinovsky had some good ideas and that "Yeltsin and Zhirinovsky understood each other. Zakhar's understanding of Zhirinovsky's ultra-nationalism was interesting:

"Look, a man belongs to where he was born or to where he spent his life.

"I, for example, was born in Ukraine of a Ukrainian mother and Russian father, but I spent my entire life either in Central Russia or in Siberia, living with the Tartars, of all people. I feel Russian, but we are all the same people. It does not matter if you are Jewish, Ukrainian, Georgian or Russian. What's the difference?"

"But it matters to Zhirinovsky," I interjected.

"Zhirinovsky," said Zakhar, "is half Jewish himself and if he speaks poorly about some Jews or Georgians or others, it's because he is right. If they don't care for Russia, their place is not in Russia. We are all the same people. There are good people and there are bad people. I like them all if they are good and they want to be with Russia. But if, for example, they are like the Moldavians, who don't want to be with us, then we don't need them. Nobody should force people to be what they are not and what they don't want to be. Nationalism is not a science; it is a feeling. Deep down, you know what you are and you also want to be with your own kind, as one would expect. If you are with your own people then even the hardest things are easier to take. That's what Zhirinovsky stands for."

As we drove through Moscow's urban decay, Zakhar began to talk about himself.

"Things are bad but they must change for the better. Somehow. My family is in the country in a *kolkhoz* [a collective farm]. Just imagine, before the Revolution there would have been a nobleman's mansion there with all kinds of riches, with the ordinary folk sweating for him and living worse than animals. But at least people lived close to the soil. Then they started this collectivization, and we forgot how to live on the soil. Before the collectivization, a child would know how to act around farm animals. We knew what the sunrise, the sunset, and the seasons meant. We lost it all in the *kolkhoz*. Farming became like a factory. And now, we are trying to reclaim the animals and the soil. A child has to be taught by his parents how to live on the soil. Parents will send him in the morning to feed the pigs and to clean the horses. Once you learn it, you miss it if you don't have it later on."

I asked Zakhar how he came to leave the *kolkhoz*. He said that he was a tractor driver and a mechanic at first, but then he decided to try his luck in a nearby town. There he became a driver for one of the local higher-ups in the party bureaucracy. One day his boss got lucky; he was transferred to Moscow and Zakhar went with him. Eventually, he became a driver for Mosfilm, where he still works.

Zakhar has a hobby. He loves to make things with his hands. He does carpentry out of love, and car mechanics and driving for a living. He treasures most the moments when he can create things with his hands.

"You can buy things," he said, "but how many things can you make yourself? Where is the pride?"

He answered the question himself.

"There is none. There are all these things that we do so poorly, so shabbily. There is no longer any pride in skills. Man should work hard and well and he ought to have pride in what he does. If he has that, then he wins respect. And if he is respected, he can reward himself."

Zakhar entered into a passionate discourse about life's pleasures. For Zakhar, the reward after a job well done is having vodka with friends. Our subsequent discussion or rather, Zakhar's lengthy monologue, became focused on issues related to vodka and Russian men.

"This Gorbachev. Why did he take vodka away from the people? That was stupid. He only hurt the working people. If you work hard all week long, you should be able to buy some vodka on Saturday and have it properly at home, at the table with food, with friends, with family. That is the right of the working man!

"When Gorbachev arrived on the scene in 1985, I liked him, but then he started these stupid reforms, like raising prices on vodka. That's when he lost me. He lost lots of working men like me. He took away the only pleasure we had."

Zakhar become so indignant that he stopped talking for a long while. I thought he had forgotten the vodka issue and asked him about something else, but he ignored my question and continued.

"The rich—the black marketeers and the mafia—they weren't affected by these new high prices of vodka. They have money anyway. But the working man got a kick in the head."

He suddenly remembered that I had asked him about Yeltsin.

"Why do you think people like Yeltsin? Because he knows that a person needs his vodka. Why did people vote for Zhirinovsky in 1993? Because he knows vodka is important. But Gorbachev and his mineral water—what a laugh! That's how he lost us."

There is no stopping Zakhar. He talks like a man with a mission.

"I have worked hard all my life," he says. "I know exactly how much I can drink, where and with whom. I am a professional driver, so I should know better than anybody. And I do. I never drink on the job. Never. I'm not a hooligan. I am a normal Russian man and that is how most working Russian men feel. Trust me.

"Before Gorbachev," he continued, "I could buy our Russian vodka in state stores and I could afford it. I don't want your whisky, your cognacs or wines; I don't like them and I don't have that kind of money. But I am made to feel like some kind of a criminal if I buy or, God forbid, drink, home-brewed vodka. It is illegal, you know, but it is the closest to the real thing and the only kind that I can afford now.

"Before, I could go to a bar for some vodka and food. I would always have a couple of bottles at home, just in case. That's all. It was a pleasure one could look forward to. Now our people drink alone on the sly—in toilets, in doorways, behind bushes, without food—like criminals. Why? What was wrong with the way it was before? Some vodka with friends, or with a meal, at home after work. Now, no pleasures are left. One works harder than ever and cannot even afford to have a drink, and if you do, you feel like a thief."

Suddenly Zakhar jammed on the brakes and our Volga screeched to a halt. Sitting in the front seat beside Zakhar (there were no seatbelts), I almost flew through the windshield. Zakhar cursed and pulled over to the side of the road. It all happened so fast that I am not quite sure what had occurred.

Zakhar, almost shouting, gave me an explanation.

"It's those bandits, the mafia! Did you see the two cars chasing each other?"

I didn't, but apparently that is what had happened. Weaving in and out of the traffic, two cars were involved in a reckless chase. Zakhar knew that they were mafia cars.

"You see, they are these new *bisnessmeny* [businessmen]. They shoot each other, they kill, maim and stab. That's this new free market, you know. There's no room for normal, honest folk. Free market! Free for whom? For bandits like them, that's for who. There is no control, the mafia are everywhere. Everybody grabs what they can, the mafia together with the reformers. May the dog spit on them! It is one thing to sell what you make with your own hands—a scarf, a doll, sausages. But if you buy it in one place, hoard it and then sell for ten times as much, then you are a bandit!"

Zakhar says it is lucky that he does not smoke.

"Ordinary people have a hard time getting Russian cigarettes in state stores, but if you go outside the store, they are all there at ten times the price! That's the free market for you. I'm outraged!"

On Sundays Zakhar and his wife visit their family who live in the country and help them work their small piece of land. In return they get some cabbage and potatoes.

"The food is a great help. I don't know how we would make it otherwise."

I asked him what he thought about privatization of the land. He thought that it was a good idea in theory but in practice it didn't work because "even if the whole family manages to obtain the money to buy the land, there is nothing left for things such as equipment, fertilizers, seeds and animals.

"And worst of all," he concludes as we approach the grounds of Mosfilm where Zakhar was letting me off, "even if you bought the land and you are doing well, the whole village will envy you and hold it against you for succeeding where they cannot. They may even burn you out, harm your stock, or destroy other property. Our people don't like to see their neighbours prosper."

While drinking, as described by Zakhar, may appear to be a relatively harmless and pleasurable social activity—the reward at the end of one's working day—statistics demonstrate that the effects of drinking in Russia are frightening. About 70 percent of the crimes in Russia are committed by people who have been drinking and about 60 percent of all deaths, accidental or otherwise, involve drinking. A recent report in the *British Medical Journal* indicates that Russian men drink a bottle of vodka every two days. In addition, an increasing number of women are drinking and the overall average age of drinkers is becoming progressively lower.

It is not known to what extent these statistics have changed over the past ten years, but what is clear is that drunkenness is far more visible than ever before.

In the past, the Labour Therapy Prevention Centres kept drunks off the street. There were 170 of these euphemistically named centres where alcoholics would be locked up and separated from the rest of society for a certain period of time. Although their effectiveness was limited in terms of therapy or rehabilitation, they kept drunks out of the public eye. The centres have all been recently closed, but the need for genuine rehabilitation centres for alcoholics is urgent.

There is an attempt to introduce the Alcoholics Anonymous program in Russia and with it a whole new way of looking at drinking problems and recovery. It is too soon to know if the program will have any degree of success, but with its emphasis on faith and collective will, it might in the long run appeal to many Russians.

Searching for New Gods

WHILE IN WESTERN SOCIETIES money is a symbol of the highest achievement and happiness for many, it is a relatively new phenomenon in Russia. Under communism, some had privilege, few had money, and even fewer could aspire to having any. And even if one had money, there was not much to buy with it.

In the new Russia all of this has changed. Though still only a few Russians have money, there are all kinds of goods to be purchased with it, and for many Russians money has became a new religion. Money emerges as the major topic of nearly every Russian's conversation. The majority of Russians with whom I spoke feel that, in all likelihood, they will never have a chance to be rich or even comfortable. And they are right, because their skills and professions do not have the promise of any money—ever. What is a teacher, a civil servant, a clerk, a librarian, an old-style administrator or manager, or a retired pensioner to do? How is an ageing skilled worker whose factory has closed going to learn new skills? What are the female sales-clerks going to do when they are fired because they are not considered attractive or young enough?

The abundance of merchandise in Russian stores is often seen as an insult, and the wealth that some people have is not considered a measure of success and a reward for hard work and talent, but rather as evidence of being a crook.

Education is now looked upon only in terms of providing the means to make money. Under communism, the individual felt himself to be a helpless victim of the totalitarian system; now he is told that anybody can be rich and that it is up to the individual to realize his potential to reach this goal. Today, Russians are made to feel that if they fail to become rich, it is their own personal failure and they alone are responsible for it.

Younger people particularly, are becoming increasingly obsessed with money and with the ways and means to make it. Money becomes the central focus of their existence.

"For the first time in our lives we have a chance to get rich now! We want to make money; we want to have things that people in the West have! That's what human rights are," two teenage punks outside a Moscow music store told me.

Asked what they thought about the elderly beggars nearby, they shrugged their shoulders.

"These people are the past, and who gives a damn, anyway. It is time for them to die."

Nearly everyone I talked with, well off or not, seems convinced that money can take care of everything. "Everything" seems to be pretty one-dimensional these days. You have problems because you have no money; if you do have money, you have another problem: how to protect it and what to do with it.

One person I encountered didn't seem to have any problem using his money and he appeared to be protecting it rather well too. I was in one of the new art galleries which have sprouted like mushrooms since 1991. This one was located near Red Square. There were paintings by established Russian painters, traditional and abstract, and they were priced in U.S. dollars. While the works were clearly intended to be bought by foreigners, there were some Russian buyers present the day I was there. I liked many of the paintings but since few of them cost less than $5,000, they were a bit too expensive for my pocketbook. In addition to paintings, the gallery carried some exquisite handcrafted silver jewellery with precious and semi-precious stones. Prices ranged from $100 to $1,000.

I was intrigued by one buyer. At first I thought he was a foreigner—a good looking, well-dressed Frenchman or Italian in his mid-thirties. Incredibly, he was finalizing the purchase of about a $100,000 worth of paintings. I had to move closer to get a better look at this rather extraordinary sale, conducted right in front of everybody in the gallery. The money was being unloaded from an elegant leather suitcase and carefully arranged in neat piles on the counter, ready to be counted. Only then did I became fully aware that the gallery was literally swarming with young, stylishly-dressed men. Some of them were the companions of the buyer and the others, I realized, were security people for the gallery. Now that my eyes were truly seeing, I noticed that they all had guns.

The buyer again caught my attention when I heard him talking with the sales people in flawless Russian. Mustering my courage, I approached the buyer, introduced myself, and asked whether I could ask him a few questions for my book. He spoke a few words in another language to his friends and a few minutes later one of the gallery's sales staff ushered us both to a secluded corner.

While he declined to be interviewed on tape, the man agreed to talk to me. He said his name was Gregor and that he was from Georgia. He had a number of businesses in Tbilisi and Moscow, on which he would not elaborate. He expressed no interest in politics and stated his credo unequivocally. "Money is my politics. Beauty is my religion. I love art and beautiful women."

He likes Russia the way it is now because he can make money. He could not care less, he told me, who is in power in Russia or in Georgia, as long as the free market has a green light. He buys art because it represents beauty and he thinks it is a good investment. Leaving Russia to live in the West, he said, was a serious consideration, but only if money-making opportunities would cease to exist in Russia.

I was clearly talking with a so-called mafia man. I was about to thank him and make my exit when one of his men came up and presented me with a little box. In it was the expensive hand-made silver necklace I had admired earlier. Gregor presented me with the necklace. When I protested and said that I couldn't possibly accept it, he became quite angry. He said it was a token of friendship and it is customary in Georgia to offer gifts in friendship. A refusal is considered insulting, so I accepted the gift and bade a hasty goodbye, but not before being offered a ride in Gregor's new red Porsche. I very politely, but firmly, declined.

I met Nina while she was visiting my friends in St. Petersburg. Nina lives in Nizhnyi Gorod, Russia's third largest city. It is situated on the Volga river, 300 kilometers east of Moscow. Nizhnyi Gorod, an important centre for Russia's military-industrial complex, was isolated from the rest of the world and off-limits to foreigners until 1991.

In the past few years, various religious movements from all over the world have established themselves in Nizhnyi Gorod. According to Nina, the most active among them is the Unification Church headed by Reverend Sun Myung Moon. Nina is involved with the sect's activities through her work as a high school English teacher.

"We teach English using materials provided by the sect."

She told me about these educational aids. She uses their literature and videos, and presentations are made to her by converts to the Unification Church from all over the world. American believers dominate the scene and there are a number of Black Americans among the performers. They talk, sing, and preach the joys of being the Reverend Moon's followers.

When I expressed surprise that these types of educational materials and practices would be accepted and approved as a part of the school's curriculum, Nina was incredulous.

"We are getting good English, the best, and also my students are learning about family values and that's very important for us."

She told me that her students are very enthusiastic about the Unification Church's practices and techniques of motivation and persuasion. The word "sect" does not have a negative connotation for Nina as it has for us in the West.

"Kids are bored with the Russian Orthodox Church; the rituals are meaningless to them because they don't relate to life around them. Moon's people live in today's world and they talk about the chaos that young people see everywhere. They also point the way out of this chaos by their own example. They come to classes with their families, or with pictures of their wives, husbands and children—they talk about joys of marital love and hard work. My students are spellbound."

These personalized lectures are frequently embellished with electric guitars, drums, costumes and colorful rituals. Nina observes that while most of the Rev. Moon's followers are from America or Germany, there are more and more Japanese and Koreans who come to Russia in a dual role: as Moon followers and businessmen.

According to Nina, Moon followers are everywhere in Russia. She told me that the Unification Church claims to have representatives in more than fifty cities and towns, involving hundreds of thousands of students.

The Russian Orthodox Church appealed to Yeltsin to curb the activities of foreign cults on Russian territory. Legislation to deal with the situation was proposed but nothing came of it.

While Moon followers appear to be very successful, they are not as visible as members of the Hare Krishna movement. I have encountered them on a number of occasions on both Moscow and St. Petersburg streets. Nina said that they are also a constant presence on the streets of Nizhnyi Gorod.

Long Live the Czars!

I WAS IN RUSSIA as millions watched Queen Elizabeth II's visit to Russia on television, in the fall of 1994. The splendor of the Queen's diamond tiara, the royal yacht Britannia, and her Rolls Royce viewed in the context of the magnificent, if somewhat fatigued, palaces of Peter the Great in St. Petersburg and the more severe but no less opulent Kremlin in Moscow, were to serve as the symbolic statement that the past is, if not forgotten, then at least forgiven.

The spokesman for the royal party expressed the wish that the visit would encourage democracy and the market economy in Russia. Yeltsin's spokesman in turn announced that the Queen's visit "turned a new page in history and looked toward the future."

It was a visit full of historical and political symbolism which reminded me of the Grand Ball of the Russian Nobility which I had attended six months earlier. To some, the Queen's visit was a bridge to the past which they held to be as important as the present and future in Russia. These are the descendants of the aristocracy and of the lesser nobility who believe that the Russian monarchy ought to be restored. Eighteen percent of all Russians, according to a recent poll conducted in thirty Russian cities, support the restoration of the czars. They fervently believe that to return to its historical heritage, Russia needs to resume its royal tradition.

In 1917 the Bolshevik Revolution toppled the 300-year-old Romanov dynasty; Czar Nicholas II and his entire family were murdered. The Romanovs were related to Britain's royal family.

In 1990, the Russian Society of Nobility was founded. Every year there is a by-invitation-only ball in Ostafayevo, formerly a nobleman's estate and now a suburb located in the southern part of Moscow. In pre-revolutionary Russia, it was the residential palace of Prince Viazemsky, one of the great Russian aristocrats. Eventually it became a sanatorium for the members of the Communist Party, and since 1989 it has housed the Museum of Russian Classic Poets.

In 1991, twenty-three-year-old Stephan, the grandson of my host, described his activities in the Society to me. He and other young descendants of Russian nobility take these activities very seriously. Stephan grew up knowing that his family tree went back some three hundred years. History was his passion, even in elementary school, and it developed into an all-consuming obsession. Stephan is presently completing his master's degree in Russian history and his goal in life is "to restore his family's rightful place in Russia's past and future."

Stephan is also active in the Pan-European Nobility Society of Russia, an offshoot of the Pan-European Union. Founded in 1922 in Vienna by the most prominent aristocratic families of twenty-five European countries, its objective is to "fight for the free and voluntary union of European states." The society's current president, His Imperial and Royal Highness Emperor Otto Von

One of the numerous nationalist demonstrations with some members
of the clergy and individuals in pre-revolutionary uniforms.

A military parade—just like under the Czars!

Hapsburg, the last descendant of the Hapsburg dynasty, was a close friend of Churchill and De Gaulle—who were both active members of the Society.

A pamphlet from the Pan-European Union given to me by Stephan states that "the members of the Union were and are committed to cultural, political, economic and military European unity; to the formation of the United States of Europe," and "to maintaining, preserving and developing Europe's best traditions and heritage."

Stephan invited me to attend several meetings of the Russian Society of Nobility. While some of the members of this society, like Stephan, are also active in the Russian Pan-European Society, these two organizations have their differences. Reflecting a centuries-old split within the ranks of the Russian nobility and intelligentsia, the Russian Pan-European Society is pro-Western and committed to the dissemination of European culture and traditions in Russia, and Russian traditions in Europe. The Russian Society of Nobility is intensely slavophile. The common denominator of both organizations is that they firmly believe that as the descendants of the aristocracy and nobility of Russia, they have the unique responsibility, duty and privilege, to lead Russia.

While both organizations profess to support market reforms in Russia (and they insist that they are committed to human rights), their interpretations of democracy differ.

To become a member of the Russian Nobility Society, you must to be able to document your nobility going back at least three generations. Members observe an internal pecking order, and careful attention is paid to hierarchy within the aristocratic ranks where some are more noble than others. Non-aristocratic sympathizers can join as "associate members," but they are not included in the inner circle or most of the activities of the Society.

The Russian branch of the Pan-European Society, however, tends to be a little more flexible in the observance of protocol and more "democratic" in assessing members' qualifications for membership.

My invitation to the Ball of the Russian Society of Nobility was to be seen as a privilege not bestowed upon me lightly and not often extended to the press or foreigners, unless they can prove an aristocratic connection.

Few of the Russian aristocrats are rich. But the relative shabbiness of their evening clothes didn't diminish the *haute* spirit of the occasion. The hundred guests were formally introduced by the master of ceremonies; titles and ranks were carefully and loudly announced. During the evening, etiquette was observed by all—the exaggerated courtliness stood out in graphic juxtaposition to the Russian reality outside.

I was introduced to the society's president, Prince Golitsyn. He told me that "Russia needs to learn the truth about the past." To this end, the society organizes lectures, exhibits, and discussion meetings open to all interested Russians.

The events take place in the former palace of Prince Dolgoruki, which, until 1991, housed the Marx and Engels Museum. Ironically, in the palace's former dungeons, aristocratic youth have set up a café where members and sympathizers regularly meet.

Prince Golitsyn believes that a hereditary constitutional monarchy where the czar's power is real and constant, would provide Russia with badly needed stability, continuity, and moral authority. Solzhenitsyn appears to subscribe to just such a vision of a future Russia.

However, there is considerable confusion as to who could become Russia's czar. Since 1918, there have been at least fifty claimants to the Russian throne. One of the leading candidates now is Prince Georgy Mikhailovich, a thirteen-year-old boy designated by his late grandfather Vladimir Kirilovitch, whose father was Czar Nicholas II's cousin. Another contender is Madrid's Prince Alexis d'Anjou de Bourbon-Conde who claims he is the grandson of the Nicholas II's third daughter, Mariya, who supposedly escaped the massacre of the Czar's family. The most recent favorite among older Russian royalists is Queen Elizabeth II's second son, Prince Andrew.

While older members of the nobility seem to prefer an extremely idyllic interpretation of Russia's past, the younger members subscribe to a more realistic assessment.

"The Bolshevik Revolution didn't take place in a vacuum. Pre-revolutionary Russian society was far from perfect. Glossing over the problems of the past will get us nowhere. But, our Russian heritage and tradition are immensely rich and deeply moral, and it is this heritage and tradition that we must restore, maintain and enrich," said Stephan, "without forgetting that we live in the end of the twentieth century and that the world today is a very different place than it was yesterday."

Russian Women: Liberated or Oppressed?

WITH THE EMPHASIS ON YOUTHFULNESS in North America and Western Europe, differences in age tend to blur. It used to be that Russian girls and women were immediately distinguishable from their Western counterparts because they looked so dull and drab. This is no longer the case. In the twenty years I have been visiting the Soviet Union, and in particular the last five years visiting Russia, I have noticed a dramatic change in the appearance of teenagers and young women. In this same period, the way older women look has changed little, whether they live in the country or in large urban centres.

In Russia, a woman's age and family status are almost always immediately apparent. Now virtually all unmarried teenage girls and young women are indistinguishable from their Western counterparts. This is a radical change from the pre-*perestroika* period when school girls had to observe a strict dress code. Russian girls and young women look Western in the extreme. To the dismay of their parents and grandparents, they wear the briefest of miniskirts, the tightest of leggings, and the skimpiest of tops. They also try very hard to be as skinny as possible by dieting religiously.

Valentina, the retired cook who used to work at Moscow University's cafeteria, is the mother of a thirty-four-year-old daughter and grandmother of a thirteen-year-old granddaughter. She expressed her opinion on this trend quite clearly. "They look like prostitutes and they starve themselves to death."

Her displeasure and discomfort with her granddaughter's generation's preferred style are shared by most women of her age and older.

Most Russian women in their mid-twenties to early thirties are married. Many of them have one child, and adhere to conventional ideas of femininity: high heels, full make-up, elaborate hair styles and dresses. They look young, pretty and very tired. They, too, try to diet but not very successfully.

Women in their late thirties and forties also appear tired. By Western standards they are chunky and look dowdy. Few from this group wear pants; most sport tight perms and are often pushy and somewhat aggressive in public. In their private lives, however, these same women are usually wonderfully warm and friendly.

Women in their fifties have the most commanding presence. It is clear that many of them played, or still play, important professional roles in Russia. Dressing in plain, uniform-like suits and dresses, their public behavior resembles that of one's feared but respected teacher. It is apparent that these women no longer attempt to play the conventional feminine role.

It is practically impossible to tell Russian women in their sixties, seventies and eighties apart. In an amazing transition, they become black and gray "babushkas"—old grandmothers.

Yet until a short time ago, these same babushkas constituted a power to be reckoned with, both within the labour market and in local politics, and they are still figures of authority within most families.

Women in Russia constitute 51 percent of the total population. Until recently, before they became the first victims of massive lay-offs, women made up 49 percent of industrial workers, 44 percent of agricultural workers, 84 percent of all health workers and 73 percent of educators. Women held 71 percent of the jobs in cultural industries. Over 93 percent of all able-bodied women in Russia were, until 1988, either working or studying. Measured against the past, it would appear that Russian women are better educated and more highly placed than ever before. It was a repeated claim of communist ideology that Soviet women had attained full equality with men as was guaranteed by each Soviet constitution from the beginning of Soviet power to its demise in 1991. This protection will no longer be in force when the new constitution is adopted; it has no guarantee.

Despite this constitutional protection, women rarely reached the upper echelons of politics, institutions or professions; instead, they dominated the lower ranks and received lower pay. While most of the teachers at the elementary and secondary level were women, most of the principals were men. Most of the doctors were women as well, but the heads of hospitals, the surgeons and the professors of medicine were virtually all men. In the academic world, despite holding advanced degrees, only about 10 percent of women reached the professorial level even though most of the lecturers were, and remain, women. In the bygone world of communist politics, women represented only 24 percent of party members and the Politburo included no women at all.

Shortly after the October Revolution in 1917, Alexandra Kollontai, a noted Russian revolutionary and champion of women's rights, stated that "each person, whether a man or woman, should have a real opportunity for the fullest and freest self-determination, and the widest scope for the development

Three young women in downtown Moscow.

and application of all natural inclinations."

The 1920s, 1930s and early 1940s were the decades when women became firmly established in the labour market in the Soviet Union, and their participation in production were taken for granted. Their professional gains were incontestable, and their role as mother and wife was considered secondary to their role as worker.

After World War II, women received different signals. Suddenly, it was their biological role as mothers that was to be the expression of their "natural inclinations." They had to move out of the labour market to make room for men returning from the war, and they had to have babies to replace the many lives that had been lost.

By the 1950s and 1960s, women were once again participating fully in the work force. For the time being there were enough babies, and the care of those babies and children was supported by the state. For that period, women in the Soviet Union not only had guaranteed employment, they also had maternity leave, maternity benefits and the moral and constitutional reinforcement of their roles as equal members of society. They were recognized as both workers and mothers. The situation, however, was not to last long.

The decade of the seventies marked the beginning of another demographic crisis and further manipulation of women in the name of fulfilling those "natural inclinations." Suddenly it became apparent that the birth rate among Russians was dramatically lower than that in the Central Asian republics. The danger of a "yellowing" of the Soviet Union was hinted at and it was up to Russian women to correct the situation; this time "natural inclinations" meant giving birth to Russian babies. From the beginning of the seventies, pressure increased on Russian women to focus more on family, reproduction, and femininity. Through repeated and insistent messages in the media, women were made to feel that it was their fault that so many marriages ended in divorce and that it was their responsibility to remedy the situation. This point in Soviet history marks the beginning of the double burden borne by the Russian woman. Her earnings were still essential to the welfare of the family but her status as a worker was diminishing. At the same time, her unpaid responsibilities—reproduction and maintaining the family physically and spiritually—increased.

Perestroika, initiated in 1985, only intensified the process. The value of women's work further decreased. With unemployment growing, women were the first to be let go—but becoming a full-time housewife was not a viable option for most women.

Talking to almost any women over forty, one finds a prevailing sentiment expressed best by Liza, a forty-two-year-old high school teacher and mother of a twenty-year-old daughter: "Women are far beyond the stage of wanting to sit home rocking their children to sleep."

While it is the need to supplement their husbands' marginal or nonexistent incomes that drives women into factories, shops and offices, there is no question that many, especially older women, work for reasons of personal satisfaction.

"Before the reforms, when my husband still had a job in a factory, it wouldn't make any difference to me how much he earned, I would work anyway," says Vera, a forty-eight-year-old factory worker who, by Western standards, looks at least sixty.

"My children are grown. What would I do sitting home all day? Now, of course, it is a different story. I tremble every day wondering if my job will be eliminated. They talk about closing the factory. What shall we do then? Nobody will give a job to a woman my age. How we will manage, I don't know."

The major concern of working women over forty is keeping their jobs. These women are preoccupied with economic survival.

Young women, however, are not so emphatic about work. When asked about her daughter's goals, Liza becomes evasive. Pressed, she admits that her daughter is a high school drop-out who has no aspirations or ambitions of any kind.

"It is this social and political turmoil that confuses the young; they do not know what to do with themselves," says Tatyana.

Women in their thirties usually work, and have husbands and small children. For them, the chief concern is how to combine the job and the time-consuming work of being wives and mothers. Life for the average young wife and mother in Russia is difficult. Where their mothers and older sisters had state assistance in the form of day-care centres, nurseries and summer camps, these women do not have the benefit of those facilities. In addition, there are far from enough laundromats, dry cleaners, repair shops and other services which most Westerners take for granted.

Where do men fit into the equation? In Russia, the Western practice of men helping in the kitchen or with the children remains a novel idea to most men and women. In fact, the majority of Russian women of all ages, do not wish their men to get involved in household duties at all. Instead, they want more services and appliances. Sharing the task of child-rearing is favored, but this too is problematic.

"Men are consumers in family life," confided Vera, a well-educated mother in her late thirties with two children.

"It is the woman who holds the family together, who not only feeds it and clothes it but also disciplines the children and provides the needed warmth and cohesion. Yes, I would like my husband to do more, but frankly I'm not sure that he ever will."

Larissa is thirty years old, the married mother of a four-year-old daughter.

"I studied a very long time, nearly twenty years, to get my Ph.D. I defended my doctoral thesis in Russian philology only last year and I was lucky enough to get a position as a lecturer at Moscow University. I wonder sometimes whether it was all worth it," she told me.

Larissa is an attractive, slender blonde, fashionably dressed, who has a passion for pretty underwear which she cannot afford. Her mother, Serafima, now sixty-five and the retired editor of *Russian Women (Russkaya Zhenshchina)*, a popular and influential magazine, was once a powerful woman. Today, she is trying to be open-minded about the changes. She welcomed *perestroika* and had warm words for Gorbachev. Like any professional in an important position, she was a Communist Party member but she now says:

"Communism, as represented by the party, is dead and the party is dead. I will never join any party ever again. But I always perceive communism as an ideology parallel to the Christian philosophy with its emphasis on social justice and equality. I certainly don't think that present day Russia and its politicians are concerned about either one. And as for women! Look at my Larissa! What kind of life awaits her?"

We were sitting in the kitchen of Serafima's two-bedroom Moscow apartment. Her husband, who died four years ago, was a professor of anthropology. Larissa is an only child. Larissa, her husband Yuri, who is an historian and also teaches at the university, and their daughter Lina live with Serafima because they don't have an apartment of their own. They consider themselves quite lucky because the apartment is large. Larissa and her mother are very close, which is typical of Russian mothers and daughters.

"I got married when I was in the last year of my studies," says Larissa, "and we had decided that it would be a good idea to have a child right away because the period during which one does research and writing allows the flexibility needed to raise the child. It turned out that it was not so easy, and if it wasn't for my mother and Yuri's parents, I don't know how we would have managed."

Larissa continues describing how hard it turned out to be—getting up at nights, waiting in line to buy food, cleaning and cooking, even with her mother's help—while writing her thesis.

"What about Yuri's help?" I ask and receive an amused look from the mother and a passionate speech from Larissa.

"I believe," she says, "that the most important objective in a woman's life is happiness in her personal life. Women, in general, are not as intellectually endowed as men are."

Her mother breaks in.

"Wait a minute, Larissa! And why not, may I ask?"

"Oh, mother, don't start again with your tales of all these great Soviet women scientists and achievers! Look at yourself! Where did it get you? You worked all your life, you sacrificed your family and now you get a pension that barely keeps you alive."

"How did I sacrifice my family; what have I deprived you of?" implores the mother.

"I think you had lots of fun in day-care centres and summer camps and that's something that Lina is going to be deprived of. Also, you are a nervous wreck right now and you are guilt-ridden and trying to be a Superwoman. I have given up trying to tell you that it is not possible."

This exchange continues for awhile and it is clear that it is not the first time that it is taking place. It is equally clear that despite an obvious closeness between the two women, they see eye to eye on almost nothing.

"I make 120,000 rubles a month (about forty dollars) and Yuri, who is also a lecturer, makes twice the amount. Yes, it is fair because as a rule, men produce better work. The majority of women, even with advanced degrees, are less concerned with professional advancement and more, like myself, with issues relating to family life, children and personal matters."

"Like fancy underwear and makeup?" interjects her mother.

"Yes, that too, and why not?" cries an exasperated Larissa.

"That's why you are not being taken seriously at work and that's why Yuri doesn't take your job too seriously either," says Serafima.

In fact, Larissa is very nervous about losing her job.

"I don't know how we would make it without my salary, even though it is so little," she says.

But she also admits that her husband views her academic goals and activities with "a good-natured irony" and doesn't take them all that seriously.

"Few women my age and younger see our jobs as our primary responsibility in life, though we think that having a job is very important. But non-professional women feel differently. They work because they need the money. The minute they could afford to give up their jobs, they would do it, and they would devote themselves to their families and children. I personally feel that society as a whole would benefit if these women could do just that: bring up their children and take care of their husbands and homes."

"Come on, Larissa, you cannot be serious!" says her mother emphatically. "Do you honestly believe that most of our women would want to live only within one's family, without any outside interests?"

"Yes, I do! Yes, I do!"

Marina is an attractive twenty-seven-year-old lawyer. She is married, has no children, and works for Moscow City Council. Her clothes are expensive, obviously Western, she is carefully made-up and slender. We are sitting in the council's cafeteria. Marina speaks slowly and thoughtfully.

"I am a woman, a professional woman, and I truly wonder what my life will be in this new order. I want to have both—a family and a profession—and yet I see more and more women losing their jobs. Women are fired first. Of course, many women are very tired and they would be happy to stay home and take care of their families, but how will they manage? There is simply not enough money if only the man works."

But if they didn't have to worry about the money, would they still prefer to stay home? Would you stay home? I ask.

"If we are speaking honestly," says Marina, "I think we have to admit that family is woman's first priority. Everything has become much harder for women now after the reforms. To get more money, women take on two, three jobs. There are no summer camps for children any more; women are falling on their faces, literally. Job security doesn't exist. It is no longer safe on the streets or on the subway. Men are angry and frustrated. They drink more and take their frustrations out on women."

We talk about politics and Marina's job, but almost inevitably, as was the case in all my talks with women, the conversation returns to the so called "personal" issues.

"I have been married for six years now," says Marina.

"I have a good man, otherwise we would not be together. We plan to have children but it is so hard to decide when to start. I have had three abortions already," she says very matter-of-factly. "My husband is an economist. We both wanted changes and we are happy that communism is dead although we don't know what the future will bring."

And then, as we are saying our final goodbyes, Marina looks at me.

"I hope you won't be offended, but I want to say one more thing. It is about your Western feminists, particularly the ones in America. I read that they are shocked by the Russian woman's reluctance to adopt the ideas of feminism. But I think they just don't understand anything about our problems and our concerns. And their problems are foreign to us as well. In fact, from our perspective, they seem downright ridiculous. You see, Russian women will never go against their men. We are in these troubles together."

I met Valentina on a train from Moscow to Sherpukhov, a small town two hours northwest of the capital. She was going to spend the week with her daughter's family. To be more precise, Valentina was going to resume her duties as baby-sitter to her grandchildren while her daughter and husband worked. It was June, school was over and there was nothing else that could be done with the two children, ten and twelve years of age, except to rent a room outside the city so the children coulde enjoy fresh air and have Valentina stay there with them.

Valentina is fifty-six, but looks much older. When I met her she was carrying some thirty kilos of foodstuffs with her so the family would have some food. "You cannot buy anything in Sherpukhov. Maybe bread, if you are lucky."

"I am retired now because I have a heart condition and varicose veins; I couldn't stay on my feet. I worked in the kitchen at the Moscow University cafeteria. I was a cook. My life was never easy; I always worked; I have raised a family—a son and a daughter. But things were never so hard for women as they are now. Women pay for all these changes, with their health, with their time, with their endless suffering. Look at our stores. Everywhere women ... waiting in lines, carrying heavy bags. I wanted changes, that much I knew.

"Before, when I worked—I retired five years ago—life made some sense. It was hard, but I had hopes for my children, for my grandchildren. Now I look at my daughter, she is a postal clerk, and I feel like crying. My life is over but she is only thirty-two and she looks like a worn-out mare. My heart bleeds when I look at her life. Her husband works at a chemical lab. He doesn't talk much about it. But you know, things are not good between them. He gets drunk because he is worried about his job and the need for more money. My Masha has already had four abortions and he just won't leave her alone. You know how men are."

Lala is in her mid-thirties and used to teach American literature at Moscow University. She is writing her doctoral dissertation while on maternity leave. She had her baby boy five months ago; her older son is ten. Her husband was a member of Moscow City Council. He was elected to be a representative of his district in 1990 and he and his wife were great supporters of the reforms and changes. Today they sound disillusioned and bitter.

"It is incredibly difficult now," says Lala.

"Nobody helps me. My husband works day and night. He comes home very late every evening. Everything—home, children, groceries, and work—is in my hands. There is no time for anything else. There are days when I feel I will go out of my mind."

Lala and Boris are Armenians but have lived in Moscow most of their lives. They both have family in Armenia and are in close contact, but they think of Russia as their home. Their older boy still speaks fluent Armenian.

The family lives in a two-bedroom apartment which, by Russian standards, is quite luxurious. By Western standards, the apartment, located in one of these faceless suburbs surrounding Moscow, is small and crowded. Boris, a classical musician by training, has a grand piano which takes up nearly the entire living room.

"We have enough money for us to survive, but not enough to buy everything we need. We eat much less meat now and I buy less cold cuts or cheese because only the most basic products are available. And every day the prices are higher and higher. It is practically impossible to buy anything other than food," says Lala.

"As far as the future goes, I have no idea how it will turn out. I don't know when or if I will get my job back. Maybe I will have to look for some work where I can use my English. But even if I get something, how shall I manage? Who will take care of the children? Day-care centres, nurseries and after-school care are coming to an end. Our parents live in Armenia and we don't have anybody to help us. If I don't bring in money, we will not survive on Boris's salary alone.

"We still have a car but we will have to sell it. We can't afford it. And to think that only a few years ago we had plans for the future and were full of enthusiasm about the changes."

Elena Ivanovna is eighty-four-years old. I was taken to meet her by Aleksei, her nephew, a writer and translator and an old friend of mine. I knew Aleksei's mother, a writer and translator herself, who died a few years ago. Elena Ivanovna is a beautiful woman. She is very cultured and well read. She was born into a family of rich merchants with liberal leanings. They lost their wealth after the Revolution but supported it nevertheless, and remained in Russia. Elena is the only living member of the family from her generation. She lives alone in a large, three-room apartment in the old, beautiful part of Moscow, her home for the past fifty-eight years.

Elena Ivanovna was a professional working woman all her life. She was a mechanical engineer in a large Moscow factory and a freelance writer for a number of Russian papers and journals. I was absolutely amazed at how well-informed she was about all the literary and artistic events taking place, both in Russia and elsewhere. Until recently, she also followed political developments very closely. Although Elena was a life-long Communist Party member, she welcomed Gorbachev's *glasnost* and *perestroika* and was supportive of changes. Now, she no longer is.

"I have lived nearly all my life under communism. I was born in 1909, so I lived a total of eight years without it. I lived through the Revolution, the Civil War (1917-1921), and through the First and Second World Wars. So many years have passed. I had my profession; I had my pride. In the past, there were times of horror and fear, but at least we knew who the enemy was."

Elena Ivanovna is overwhelmed by emotion, but continued.

"Today I am terrified, absolutely terrified by everything that is happening. My life is over, and there is no future for me. We, the old people, are humiliated and cast aside. Our pride and dignity are taken away. Our beliefs are spat upon. Our pensions condemn us to starvation. I have only one thing left: my family. Everything else has no meaning and it is horrible to live this way."

Forward to the Past: The Price of Femininity

IF LIFE IS HARD for young married women and for older women, it is at least a life with no delusions. For Russian teenage girls and young unmarried women, life seems to be one great illusion. This group truly doesn't know who the "enemy" is, as Elena put it. I met with some of these young women, quite by accident, as it turned out, and what I learned astonished me.

The meeting had been arranged informally by friends from Moscow University. There was supposed to be a group of about fifteen young men and women from different departments meeting with me to "talk about everything" for about an hour. Somehow, messages got crossed and in the end I met with eighteen female students. We spent three hours together, my tape running. I asked questions about politics, reforms, economy and religion and received some fascinating insights. These young women wanted to talk about the issues of greatest importance to them: male-female relations, family, children, and sex.

All the girls were between eighteen and twenty-two except for one twenty-nine-year-old graduate student. In appearance, they were virtually indistinguishable from North American students aside from the fact that they wore more makeup. They had long hair and wore blue jeans or miniskirts with body-fitting or loose tops. At first, they were more shy than their Western counterparts would have been in a similar situation. However, they quickly forgot the tape recorder and became so excited by the discussion that I lost track of who was saying what. I let it be and allowed the interview to become a free-wheeling, spontaneous, sometimes stormy conversation. The girls said that they had never before spoken like that in a group of their peers.

To begin the discussion, I introduced myself, showed pictures of my family and home and told them a bit about my own background and interests. In the three hours that followed, I found them to have a certain degree of political sophistication, only a passing interest in politics and an outlook on their anticipated roles as women which ranged from the naive and idealistic to the astoundingly conventional—definitely different from the outlook of their mothers and grandmothers.

"The Soviet system and communist ideology," said Natasha, nineteen, "disregarded human nature, and nature is the most important factor. Nature is destiny for women."

"Right," picked up Masha, twenty. "By nature, women are not meant for politics."

Both girls are political science majors.

"Nonsense," countered Mariya, twenty-nine, the only graduate student in the group. She quotes some current statistics according to which only 17 percent of female Moscow University students plan to work professionally.

I asked them what is the point of their being students if they do not plan to work. Most of them declare that they want to help their future husbands in business or politics rather than have jobs themselves. Mariya, it turns out, is the only self-proclaimed feminist in the group and she tells them that they assume they are going to have a choice whether or not they work. The others reply that given the choice they would all rather stay home and have babies. Some add that perhaps they would like to work part-time, but that "the primary attention ought to be given to husband and children."

"But you all know that the man's salary alone is not enough to support the family," said Mariya.

"Well, that's why we will have to work for a while until it gets better," the girls retort.

"Don't you realize that 75 percent of all people laid off these days are women?" shouts Mariya.

"Oh, but they are mostly older women. It will be different for us," said Tanya, twenty. "I hope to find a husband who will be already established and have some position and money, so I can have his children and assist him to to make his life smooth and comfortable at home."

They all want to have families and children. Masha wants to have three children and a husband involved in politics. "I will stay home and take care of the family, but whenever my husband needs me in politics, I will be there to support him."

"Who will take care of these three children?"

"Oh, my parents will; they can't wait to have grandchildren."

"You are so naive, Masha," said Mariya.

"So, what will you do, if you are so smart, Mariya?"

"I will work. I don't really know yet what I want and how I want it. I see our mothers and grandmothers and I see all the lies regarding the equality they supposedly had, but I also know that I could not just sit at home and be my husband's little maid."

"Well, maybe you will become Russia's first woman president," I said.

"No, I don't think a woman from our generation will be president. We are not ready for it. Nor are our men."

"Right!" jumped in the others. "It is not in the Russian tradition for women to rule. Women might be behind the men who rule, but no men will take orders from women."

"What about Catherine the Great? Is there a Catherine the Great in this room?" I asked.

"No's" came from every direction. "You see, when we think of Catherine the Great, we think mostly in terms of her sexual power over men. And we do not see her as feminine or happy. A happy, fulfilled woman in Russia is not a woman who takes like Catherine did. A woman should give."

A lone voice disagrees.

"No, I don't quite agree. We have a tradition of strong women and weak men. Look at characters in our literature and in life. Look around. It is always the woman who carries the burden of just about everything on her shoulders."

"Yes, but our strength means we have to support our men. The point is to restore their faith in themselves and not to emasculate them by displaying our strength. A strong woman should be smart enough to be weak. That's what my mother says."

"I, for one, would never listen to my mother," said Nadia. "I don't want to be like my mother. Don't you see? She is forty-five, a doctor. She worked all her life and is old, divorced, and unhappy. My mother says her life is over and hates everything that is happening."

"You know, my mother is forty and pretty miserable too, but I really envy my grandmother. She is pretty cool. She never had any doubts about who she is, or was. My grandmother is seventy years old now and, of course, she hates everything that has happened to the Soviet Union, but before that she was happy. She was an engineer in a large enterprise; she was a big wheel. She says that surviving World War II made her understand where the priorities in life are and she misses the past very much," recounted Tanya.

"The real answer to all our problems is to find a rich husband. Our girls would do anything to get a rich husband," said Masha.

"Oh, but where to find them?"

"Foreigners are the best bet! There are special agencies, ads in newspapers, a whole industry designed to locate rich foreign husbands for Russian girls."

"Would you do it?"

"No, not us, but we all know girls who do or want to do it."

"Another way is prostitution."

"Prostitution?"

"Yes, we all know students who became prostitutes, both to make some money and, possibly, to meet a rich, future husband."

I asked about the new image of Russian women seen in the media and what they thought about the flood of sexually-explicit literature that can be found everywhere.

"Most of the men I know love it."

"Oh, many women do too. They think it's all very glamorous."

"You know, Russia used to be always so puritanical and hypocritical about sex and sexuality. So now we have gone to the other extreme."

"Why extreme? It's fun to be sexy!"

"No, it's degrading!"

"What's so degrading about your body?"

"You mean, you like it the way women's bodies are shown in those dirty magazines in the subway stations?"

"Well, maybe not in all of them, but there are some magazines like *Playboy* that are nice. Surely it is okay to look nice, to have pretty things, to be attractive."

"Yes, but don't you see? Our men are comparing us to Western models and pin-ups. And how can we ever look like that? Those girls are so skinny."

Yes, that's true. Few of us are built that way and that's why so many girls are starving themselves, especially teenagers. My little sister says she will kill herself if she gets hips and breasts."

"Do you think young Russian men want you to look like these Western models?" I asked.

"Oh yes, many of them do. Many of our men want a woman to be just an ornament."

"Is that what you want to be?"

"Well, girls don't think like that. They think that they will remain young and attractive if they take good care of themselves. It is a woman's duty to take care of herself and it is her own fault if she lets herself go," said Nadia.

"All this emphasis on beauty, pornography and sex is not freedom but exploitation of women," Mariya adds.

"You see, we went from one extreme of the nineteenth-century ideal woman, all spiritual force devoid of flesh and sexuality, to the communist model of woman the comrade, all muscles and brain, to the present image of woman as a plaything, all flesh, sexually-ready and submissive."

"You are right, Mariya. What we want to be is a woman—a human being, but it should be a matter of individual choice. We should be able to be what we want to be, right?"

Since all the girls were unmarried, I ask them about their boyfriends and how they view their relationships. It turns out, as some girls shyly admit, that it is not easy for most of them to date. How come?

"Well, there is this thing about sex. Our parents would never talk about it. They are embarrassed," said Natasha. "There wasn't much said about it at school either. We have to learn about it from each other. Don't get us wrong. We know the facts of life," said Tanya, and the girls giggle. "The problem is something else."

There is a long silence; the girls are clearly embarrassed.

"You see, it is easier if you are already married. When you date, there is a problem with contraceptives."

"You mean they are still hard to get?"

In the past, before *glasnost* and *perestroika,* contraceptives were not easily obtained and the most common method of birth control was abortion. An average Russian woman would have five to eight abortions by the time she reached forty. Abortions were free and performed on demand in state hospitals.

"Well," said the girls, "one can buy condoms now, but it is not easy."

"Why?"

"It's embarrassing. No woman would go and ask for a condom. And abortions are not so simple when you are not married and live at home."

"Wait a minute," I said. "I don't follow. Why can't you use the pill, or IUD, or ask your boyfriend to get some condoms if you are embarrassed?"

"We are afraid of the pill, IUDs are not popular with our doctors, and we can't ask our boyfriends to get condoms."

"Why not?" I asked again.

"Condoms are a no-no. Men don't like them."

The girls all talk at once now.

"All the men I know don't like to use condoms."

"Guys just refuse to use them."

"They say it is unnatural!"

"It is a serious problem with Russian men. They just won't do it. And all the girls I know would not dream of demanding that they do. I wouldn't."

"Most women feel that if they demand that their boyfriend use a condom, they seriously risk losing him. He can easily find another girl who won't make such 'unnatural demands' on him."

"Men say that sex is much less pleasurable with a condom. We always end up giving in and then we die of worry every month if our periods are late."

"Yes, men say it is a woman's job to take care of such things and, if all else fails, there is always abortion."

"What about AIDS and STDs, don't you worry about that? Don't you worry that you could lose your life because of unprotected sex?"

The girls admit that they don't really see it quite this way. The reality of AIDS, in particular, has not sunk in. And while there is some mention of these issues in the media, the prevailing majority of young and old alike do not believe it concerns them.

When I asked them if there was a moral aspect to abortion, they didn't seem to understand what I was talking about.

"My mother would never talk about all the abortions she had in any detail, but she never made a secret of the fact that she had them."

"It's just something you do when you have to."

"It's a part of being a female. You endure it."

"It hurts and it can get messy if not done right."

"What can you do? Men need sex more than we do but we need men more than they need us," said Natasha cryptically. Other girls nod and I ask them for clarification. They start explaining and some new issues emerge.

"We need men, boyfriends more than ever before. There is such horrible crime now. You just don't leave home in the evening by yourself unless you absolutely have to. You desperately need a man to protect you," said Valya.

"That's true," Mariya backed her up.

"You are frightened to go anywhere alone. How can one talk about equality and independence or professional life if you know it is dangerous for a woman to be alone outside after dark?"

"Yes, you will do anything to have a guy. Without him you have no life!"

I tell them that crime and especially crime against women is also a serious problem in North America, and their reaction to my statement is unexpected.

"Don't make us laugh! What you are saying shows that you, like all women in the West, do not understand our realities at all! We see all these Western and American films, with your women getting into their cars and driving wherever they need to. You may have crime but you can get from place to place in safety. We cannot. We all have to use public transportation, and walk down dark streets. It is very dangerous now.

"That's something we envy about our mothers and grandmothers. They were safe! The way things are now, it seems like suddenly women are the prey. It is permissible to attack them. Like they asked for it. And it seems that if they are alone, they belong to no one and to everyone. That's why you need a man and you have to do everything to get him."

Women as Agents of Change

SINCE I BEGAN INTERVIEWING RUSSIANS for this book in 1991 I have noticed a significant change in attitudes—an evolution perhaps. Between 1991 and 1993 there was a notable absence of political and politically-active women in the interviews that I conducted. In the summer of 1994 1 couldn't help but observe the emergence of a great many such women, due in part to their election to the Duma in December, 1993.

It is a dramatic development and I believe that it is the most significant change in Russia during the last year—a change hardly observed by the Western media.

Women, mostly between the ages of thirty-three and forty-six are organizing on an unprecedented scale. It is the most genuine grassroots movement in Russia since the beginnings of *perestroika* in 1985. 1 believe that it is a movement which will affect every facet of Russia's future development to a much greater extent than any previous social, political or economic process.

One arm of the women's movement is Russia's leading women's newspaper, *Moskvichka (Muscovite Woman),* founded five years ago in Moscow by a group of journalists who believed that there was an urgent need for such a newspaper.

I met with *Moskvichka's* editor, Victoria Arseyevna, a woman in her early fifties, wife and mother and, first and foremost, a woman totally committed to the cause of women. We talked about the newspaper, about Russian women and about values.

"Above all, we want to express the soul of Russian women. We are extremely concerned with values—ethical, spiritual and religious. We are against vulgar commercialization and Westernization because we think they destroy the basic humanity and souls of our people."

The paper's main objective is to provide Russian women with a sense of solidarity, to make them realize that they share the same hardships, aspirations, pain and hopes. It attempts to provide a forum where women can verbalize their feelings, express their wishes and needs, and raise their political consciousness. *Moskvichka* concerns itself with everyday life as it pertains to women, their families and jobs. But it also emphasizes the importance of active politics and of the Russian Orthodox religion. Readers and contributors are mostly educated, professional women over thirty years of age—lawyers, teachers, filmmakers, administrators, politicians, economists, accountants, engineers, businesswomen and homemakers.

"Our readers and contributors are obviously very well informed," says Victoria Arseyevna. "They are also, for the most part, very committed to action."

Arseyevna believes that the emergence of such committed women taking an active interest in politics and in grassroots organizing will have a great impact upon the future of Russia.

Before *perestroika,* under communism, any political activities involving women were purely symbolic since women had very little political power whatsoever and all women's organizations and publications served as mouthpieces for the official party line.

I asked Victoria if the life of women was better or worse under communism and she said that even though it is a very complex question, one must say that it is better now. When I asked her to elaborate, she said:

"There is an enormous struggle going on in Russia now. Under communism, it was simple. Women carried a double burden—work and family. In theory there was supposed to be equality; in reality, everybody knew there wasn't. Now, there is no theory to speak of and there is this immensely difficult and complex reality. Many women say that before *perestroika* they knew who the enemy was and now they don't. It is particularly elderly women who lost everything, and the very young women who are so confused. Before, there was no choice. We can now make moral choices and we can act politically if we make such choices. We must. And we do."

What Victoria said about young and old women echoed my own impressions and findings over the past three years. Her statement about the choice and political participation signaled a direction that was altogether new.

In December 1993, sixty-nine women from various political parties were elected to the Duma. They represent 16 percent of the Duma's 425 deputies. These women speak on the pages of *Moskvichka*. Remarkably, more often than not, they vote as a block on most issues, regardless of their party affiliation. Arseyevna is very happy about this and is optimistic about this new solidarity among women.

So if there is a new type of politics emerging in Russia, it is the women's profile that is the strongest. Even though only one party—Women of Russia—addresses the so-called women's issues, women voters and female deputies from the other parties clearly got the message. *Moskvichka* was the only Russian paper that took the Women of Russia party seriously before the December 1993 elections and formally endorsed its political platform.

Moskvichka addresses the issues of women's everyday life and the so-called big issues, such the protection of the numerous gains that women had achieved under communism.

As Victoria Arseyevna put it:

"Let's not get carried away with Westernization. Let's not change into feather-brained, skinny Barbie dolls. We did accomplish quite a bit under communism—women attained education and some constitutionally-guaranteed rights. Let's not allow these rights to be scattered and lost. Let's not forget human dignity and the dignity of womanhood. And let's prevent our young women and girls from becoming sexual playthings for men, beings without rights or the will to be their own persons."

I asked Victoria to explain more precisely what she meant by the dignity of womanhood.

"I am not pointing a finger at anyone in particular, but the fact is that the extremes taking place now diminish human dignity, and women are affected more than men. Of course, it is the influence of all these Western magazines and the impact of television and Western films. Be young, be beautiful, be sexy. It is a very powerful indoctrination and this country has been bombarded with this type of indoctrination for nearly ten years now. But women are beginning to wake up. Those who were eighteen years old when *perestroika* started are now twenty-eight. They have begun to see that life is not as it is depicted in Western magazines, television or movies. They are waking up and finding these images of womanhood demeaning," said Victoria Arseyevna.

She continued talking about a clear need for deeper spiritual, religious and ethical values. While people argue about politics or are cynical or apathetic about it, and, while many question economic reforms or their implementation, only a very few question the need for spiritual renewal. Women are leading the way in this direction.

"It is clear now," said Victoria, "that there is a struggle going on between two different sets of values. One value system, capitalism, is characterized by economic extremism, commercialization of every sphere of life; exploitation of the weak; lack of respect for the elderly, women and children, and sexual exploitation of women. The other is one that would combine respect for human beings within a workable economic structure."

Victoria sees women in the forefront working toward such a system. She believes that is where they have a job to do.

"It will be a system which will incorporate our religion—the Russian Orthodox faith—and spiritual values, our deepest feelings as mothers," said Victoria.

And that's why she believes women have such a profound political role to play in Russian politics. She also believes that Russian women are uniquely prepared to play such a pivotal role because they are better educated than women elsewhere in the world, and because they are becoming desperate. For the first time, women are realizing that they have the freedom to choose and act politically. Indeed, they have enormous political power.

"Today, the situation in Russia is horrifying, yet I am an optimist," said Victoria. "One cannot tell where the criminal element begins and where it ends, who is governing and who follows the orders of the mafia. It is a world ruled by men and such a world can only lead to the disintegration of Russia. But luckily, we did succeed in developing a democratic political process and, this is having some impact upon the fate of Russia. Women are beginning to

The Committee of Soldiers' Mothers of Russia was founded in 1989 to protect the human rights of young soldiers in the Russian army.

know that, and the December 1993 election demonstrated it."

It is a fact, that before the election took place, women candidates were frequently the objects of ridicule and virtually nobody took them seriously. Nobody, that is, except the voters. They have gained new respect. Right, left, and centre have tried to coerce these women deputies, but they continue to hold their own. Victoria Arseyevna believes that their power will grow.

"It will be a slow, gradual process, but it will gain strength and momentum. Gentle democracy. That's what Russian women want!"

Reading *Moskvichka* provides a diversified picture of Russian women's lives. The reader becomes familiar with issues ranging from family, children, love and men, to education, health, jobs, the economy, politics, law, the arts, and history.

Within the newspaper there are separate mini-papers that address specific interests such as cooking, gardening, fashion, English lessons and book reviews. And not forgotten are horoscopes, an advice-to-the-lovelorn column, beauty tips and marriage counseling, now found in nearly every Russian paper. What's new and breaking every Russian taboo, is a discussion of female menopause. Traditionally perceived as "the end of it all" and always treated as a shameful subject, menopause is introduced in *Moskvichka* as "one of the stages in a woman's life that should be approached naturally and openly." This is a mini-revolution.

There is also a page paid for by the International Marriage Agency. This is a page with a twist. The photographs are not those of women wishing to marry foreigners, but of men seeking Russian wives. Most of them are from Germany, Belgium, Holland, and England, with a few from the United States and Canada. From the pages of *Moskvichka* one also learns about its readers. Those with jobs and families, others jobless and alone, experience both the positive and adverse effects of the changes in Russian society. Some of the readers have adult children, many are divorced. Many have discovered that in the face of great changes in both their personal and professional lives, they are faring better than the men. They seem to adapt and to assimilate better than their male counterparts. Knowing that youth and beauty do not last, they do not buy the Western myths that these are a woman's main selling points, myths that so powerfully captivate today's younger Russian women. Instead, from the pages of *Moskvichka* emerges an altogether different type of women— fierce and fearless. These women feel that they have nothing to lose and everything to gain. They are fighters.

"Woman produce life; the future of Russia depends upon Russian women," are public statements made by some politicians. Statements such as these are perceived by *Moskvichka's* readers as phony and hypocritical because, they feel, if women are indeed so important, why do these same politicians ignore issues that affect children, women and families in their political platforms? And who can ensure that traditional contributions of women to society as mothers, homemakers and guardians of the family values, are protected?

Women and women alone, say *Moskvichka's* readers and contributors. If women themselves underestimate their role and importance, society will not value them either. Today in Russia, men talk about the importance of family, while pushing women out of jobs and eliminating the social advantages they had under communism. As a result, women are isolated, burdened with the responsibilities of children and trying to survive without jobs or resources. How does that relate to their 'importance'? asks *Moskvichka*. Women have to learn to unify; they have to form networks of women; they must to realize their power outside the family.

Now that the vote means something, women have to learn to use it, both as voters and as candidates. Over 50 percent of all voters are women and *Moskvichka* believes that its role is to make women aware of their potential power.

The women active in Russian politics, much like the readers of *Moskvichka,* are in their thirties and forties. For the first time since the October Revolution and the advent of communism, women are acting as a block in a democratically-elected body. In the Duma's upper and lower houses there are twice as many, proportionally speaking, as there were at any point in any Soviet-era legislation where, officially, women were considered equal. These women belong to different political parties: Women Of Russia-21 deputies; Zhirinovsky's Liberal Democratic Party-5; Russian Communist Party-3; the others are distributed almost evenly among the remaining six parties.

Forty-four of the women deputies (66%) are aged 33 to 46. The remaining 25 are older. All but one of the 69 deputies have a university education and most come from management, education and health fields. There is not a single worker or agricultural worker among the women deputies.

Galina S., a professor of sociology at the Russian Academy of Management and the president of a scientific research consulting company, gave me her thoughts on their distribution.

"It is not very democratic, that's true, but one is not born to be a political leader. One becomes one. And there are indications that women factory workers and peasants are becoming a significant force in grassroots organizing throughout the whole of Russia."

Women became involved and organized mostly around the so-called life issues or women's issues. But public opinion in Russia is still quite divided on the role of women in politics. While women appear to be most involved with the specific problems and questions relating to family, women, children, the elderly and social outcasts, many men wonder if these women's issues do not conflict with the 'issues of Russia.'

"It is not a new attitude and, unfortunately, it's a common one. What is Russia?" she passionately asks.

"Russia means women, children, families; it also means men. All are interested in political stability, economic solvency and security, internal and external."

Nevertheless, according to Galina, the interests of women workers, homemakers and mothers have been under-represented and undervalued over the past decade. "The so-called women's politics are the most legitimate and appropriate type of politics and women ought to, and will, continue to be profoundly involved in them," she says.

The fundamental responsibility of women deputies is to press for family legislation and for policies which, at present, are virtually nonexistent.

Article 3 of the December 1993 Constitution states: "Men and women have equal rights and freedoms and equal opportunities for their realization."

Galina suggested that such equality exists on paper only and that in order for it to become a reality, various policies relating to every sphere of life will have to be introduced.

"The fact is," she said, "there have been no positive changes in women's lives since 1985. On the contrary, new problems were added to the old ones: unemployment, a lower standard of living and quality of life, and a crisis of values, including those that relate to the family."

Indeed, the numbers and facts that the sociologist cites support this statement. To start with, 72 percent of all the unemployed in Russia are women.

"Russia is a unique country where formal democracy comes into open conflict with a very undemocratic reality," she said. In Russia today, 34 percent of all families with one child under sixteen, live below the poverty level; 42 percent of families with two children, and 70 percent with three or more children. Their poverty is caused mostly by women's inability to get jobs. Obviously, with such a situation, women's employment is the major issue. Galina does not see this situation as comparable to women's unemployment in the West even if figures might be similar.

"In Russia," she said, "virtually all women were working up to 1985. They became unemployed after many years of professional or skilled work; most of the unemployed women in Russia have a university education."

The second enemy, as seen by women, is the advocacy of private medical care voiced by many doctors.

"It is," in Galina's opinion "a path toward the death of the nation. I cannot look without shame and pain to see people begging on the streets with posters saying 'Please help me get enough money to have surgery.'"

The third most urgent issue is the spread of drugs, especially among Russian youth.

"Now is a time for women deputies, trusted by millions of voters, to raise their voices against the spread of drugs, against the genocide of Russia," says Galina.

The issue of education and the problem with its steady decline are also a concern of the women deputies.

"We have just a little power but to be really in power, we should have at least 50 percent representation in the Duma and not a mere eighteen. But, we are unified and it is just a beginning," Galina concluded.

Tamara Chepasova, a deputy and deputy head of the Labour and Social Support Committee of the Duma, is in her forties. She is married and has two grown-up children. Tamara is an engineer and economist with fifteen years experience in machine construction and eight years with management. We meet and talk in the Duma's cafeteria.

"I know why I am in the Duma," says Tamara. "I'm very pragmatic and I represent the consumer."

She continues.

"Not everyone ought to be involved in politics, only those men and women who have both the specific experience and interest. The old premise that one's ideological convictions are the major consideration for political involvement no longer holds and I consider it wrong. Politics should be practical and the politicians should serve their constituencies, not their dogmas or ideologies."

Tamara is an optimist. She does not believe different political parties ought to divide the Duma.

"Parties differ, just as the people do," she said "but they all ought to have Russia's best interests at heart and be pragmatic."

Even though Tamara represents the radical reformers party—Russia's Choice—she identifies with the issues put forward by the Women of Russia Party and votes with them on most occasions. Tamara, along with the eight other women deputies from different parties, originates from the regions rather than from Moscow and St. Petersburg, where most of the other women deputies were elected. She formed a group within the Duma called New Regional Politics, because she feels that Russia is not big cities alone and that the regions require far greater attention than they are receiving.

Another woman representing not just regional Russia but an ethnic minority as well, is Kara-Kys Arakchaa. She is from Siberia and her people are known as Tuvins (similar to the Inuit of Canada's North). Kara-Kys is in her early forties, a chemist by education, and the head of the Siberian section of the Russian Academy of Science. She is also a mother and the grandmother of a little girl.

"We are driven not by ambitions but by needs," she said "and that is what distinguishes us the most from our male politicians."

Kara-Kys Arakchaa ran for the Duma on a platform of rights for minorities. She feels that the new Constitution does not sufficiently address these issues. She continuously wrestles with the question: Should women's issues or minorities' issues be her primary concern? Compromise seems to be the only solution.

"Sadly, our male legislators all too often consider women's issues to be extremely threatening, and anything with the word 'woman' in it is bad," she said.

"I am a woman first and Tuvinka second," she added. "But we are tired, physically and morally, because we constitute only about 18 percent of the Duma. I am absolutely sure of one thing: if there were more of us in the Duma, it would be far more effective and there would be better results," Kara-Kys Arakchaa concludes.

Nadezhda Bikalova is an economist in her early forties, single, and the author of some thirty-five economic studies. She is a deputy from Chuvashkia Autonomous Russian Republic (one of the Russian Federation's republics, located in Siberia).

"In Chuvashkia," begins Nadezhda, "probably more abortions are performed per capita then in any other place in the world. That's a dubious honour. What is it, if not a slaughterhouse leading to my nation's genocide?" she exclaims.

"As one of my female voters told me, 'I am a single mother. I didn't plan it this way. It happened. But can my daughter survive on my income?' This woman had her child. Most other women choose abortion."

Nadezhda feels that one can debate politics for days, pass laws and spend time on committees, but it all amounts to very little if the laws are not respected by those holding governmental positions. This is something she observes every day.

"People come and go without being accountable to anyone; without having to explain or justify anything. All these government officials are sitting pretty. They form institutes and foundations. They organize joint ventures, and travel to America using taxpayers' money. And meanwhile, here in Russia lawlessness reigns" said Bikalova.

"I support reforms and privatization, but I am deeply disappointed with the process. Our privatization changed into privhvatization." (This is a play on words; with one letter changed, the word becomes grabbing or robbing.)

"Our budget is drained of millions which ought to be spent on social needs. I have spoken about these issues so many times but I've been ignored. That's why I decided to run for the Duma," explained Nadezhda.

"I competed against twelve male candidates and I ran on the platform 'Women of Chuvashkia for social justice.' And now, the other women and I are deputies. We all think alike. It is essential for us to be united and to be heard.

We are not as influential yet as we would wish to be because there are still too few of us. In addition, the media do not cover us in the most objective way because, even though our press is quite free, it does, nevertheless, have financial and political dependencies and obligations influencing its coverage and thus creating bias."

Evgeniya Tishkovskaya, in her mid-forties and single mother of two adopted daughters, is a petroleum engineer and financial economist. (It is not unusual for Russians to have two advanced degrees in different fields.)

"It is silly to make chicken soup with a hen that lays golden eggs," said Evgeniya, talking about Russia's budding private enterprises and the excessive taxation system that often kills them. For example, her petroleum products factory pays 93 percent of its profits in taxes! "How can such a factory function? It defies logic!" she exclaims.

Canada and the Scandinavian countries are models for Evgeniya in terms of how successful they are in resolving and dealing with social problems. She believes that women should stand united in the Duma and in politics on every level. What's more, she sees it as a primary goal to increase the number of women in parliament.

"We represent 53 percent of the total population; we should have the same percentage in the Duma" she stated emphatically.

Tatyana Nesterenko, the married mother of two daughters, is thirty-five years old. As an economist, she worked for thirteen years in Chukhotka (the far North) in financial administration. She firmly believes that Russia needs law and order, although representing women's interests and working for their unity are her chief objectives. Since she herself comes from the far North, she is especially keen on the issues pertinent to the women of her region and that includes various groups of minority women.

Forty-year-old Lyubov Rozhkova is a lawyer who heads the Educational Committee of the Duma, and sees her role primarily as a defender and promoter of fair, equal, and free education for all, something, she points out, that "is no longer any of these things under the new order."

She believes that women play an especially important role in the area of education, not only because so many women work in education, but also because they are mothers who "bear the main responsibility for their children's future."

Russian feminists—are they different from Western-style feminists? The answer is, yes, they are quite different.

Before Gorbachev's *perestroika* had begun in 1985, the words 'women's lib,' had, at best, a ridiculous, and at worst, an offensive meaning for most Russian women regardless of age or background. They were "these rich North American women," who castrated their men, who burned their bras and worse.

Following *perestroika,* with the availability of information and freedom of the press, women's liberation became a non-issue. Men and women in Russia had, it seemed, other things to worry about. It was clear that the Western concept of women's liberation was alien to Russian women.

But already at the beginning of the 1990s, it was becoming increasingly clear that women were being shortchanged by the new "democracy and free market" reforms. In 1991, the Moscow Centre for Gender Studies was founded. The first of its kind in Russia, it attracted women of great caliber such as Ludmilla Zavadskaya, a senior Russian sociologist, former advisor to Gorbachev, and a member of the Women of Russia Party. With assistance and sponsorship from various Western women's groups and organizations, the Centre began to conduct numerous studies and to organize International Forums.

The latest study conducted by the Centre established that women have been considerably left behind. While 60 percent of industrial workers are employed by the lucrative private sector already in place, only 25 percent of these workers are women. In fact, the majority of women still work in the state sector which pays very low wages, and these women will soon be unemployed.

Every year since it was founded, the Centre organizes an International Forum. Along with Western sponsors, Russian women's groups from various regions, of differing outlooks and politics, get involved. At the 1992 Forum, it was decided that the Forum would transform itself into the International Women's Organization, free of hierarchical structure and committed to the continuous exchange of information based on the development of a Women's International Information Network. It was an explicit acknowledgment of the importance of developing international programs for cooperation among women and women's organizations, and of the need to make the public aware of the problems that the elderly and very young Russian women, in particular, are experiencing.

The participants discussed numerous examples of sexual discrimination and sexism present in every aspect of Russian life. The Minister of Labour was quoted as saying: "Why should we try to find jobs for women, when men are idle and on unemployment? Let men work and women take care of the home and family."

Women were angry.

"Democracy and a free market without women—over half of the

population—is not a democracy!"

Anastasya Posadskaya, the director of the Moscow Centre for Gender Studies, pointed out that while communism clearly did not result in true emancipation of women, it proved clearly that the sexes cannot be liberated if individuals are not liberated first. Ten years of *perestroika* demonstrated beyond the shadow of a doubt that democratization of Russian society is strictly a man's affair and women are treated as objects and are not benefiting from social and economic reforms.

Woman after woman at the 1992 Forum presented evidence of the feminization of poverty in Russia, and of job discrimination, where youth and beauty are expected and often demanded. This is particularly the case in the free-market sector which narrows down its need for women to three occupations: secretary, cleaning woman or nanny. Women talked about the political barriers that must be overcome and of the propagation of the concept of "the natural destiny" of women as mothers, with the simultaneous massive exploitation of their sexuality.

Under the influence of the Centre for Gender Studies, Moscow State University, for the first time in Russia, introduced a course called Women and the Modern World.

"It is a beginning," said some of the Centre's workers, "but a very slow one. We have a long, long way to go."

PART THREE

Politics and Economics

A communist demonstration in Moscow in the shadow of Karl Marx. Lenin's portrait and red banners are in evidence, but a summer downpour forced the demonstrators to replace most of their banners with umbrellas.

Communism

MOST NORTH AMERICANS are under the impression that communism is finished in Russia. Boris Yeltsin, addressing the United States Congress in June 1992, declared:

> The world can sigh in relief; the idol of communism, which spread social strife, enmity and unparalleled brutality everywhere, which instilled fear in humanity, has collapsed... I am here to assure you that communism is dead and we shall not let it rise again in our land!

North Americans are wrong. Yeltsin is wrong.

In 1994, the communists are again the largest organized political force in Russia. Communism, although diminished in size, seems alive and well.

The communist era began in Russia in 1917. There were two revolutions in that year: the democratic revolution that took place in February, and October's Bolshevik coup, known as the October Revolution by every man, woman, and child in Russia. And while the democratic February Revolution lasted only eight months, the Bolshevik revolution encompassed over seventy years of communist rule.

In the West, we talk with ease about the oppression, horror and excesses of communism during this period. Yeltsin's proclamation of communism's demise only reinforces our conviction that every Russian must feel this way too. However, this is far from the truth.

Why is it that despite the horrors and oppression, the labour camps and executions, the lack of freedom and material comforts, so many Russians still mourn the death of communism? Why do so many seem to want it back? And why did so many Russians vote for various communist parties in the 1993 election, giving them the largest political block in the Duma? Who are these Russians?

Most supporters of today's communist parties (yes, there are more than one) are over sixty years of age, and are on pensions which pay the equivalent of $30 per month, an amount insufficient for survival. They represent approximately 20 percent of the Russian population.

Valentina is a fifty-seven-year-old cook who never was a Communist Party member and never thought of herself as a communist.

"People like me, the ordinary folk, not communists, cannot get used to the idea that everything we grew up with was bad—Lenin, Stalin, communism. Of course, we didn't know many things. The authorities kept the truth from us. We didn't know about the labour camps, we didn't know how high-on-the-hog our leaders and their families lived. I was born in 1938 and I grew up believing that the Soviet Union was a great country. Now that everything is out in the open, we realize we were lied to in many ways. It feels like we are very sick, yet we didn't even know there was this disease within us."

Valentina talked to me about her life and her family.

"What do I say to my six-year-old granddaughter when she comes to me and asks questions about Lenin?" she wondered.

"I don't know what to tell her. I cannot accept that he was a monster. I cannot accept that everything I learned and lived with and believed in was a lie. That's not right. My mother, who is eighty-one years old, still loves Stalin and believes in communism. She thinks that everything that is happening now is the work of Russia's enemies and funded by the West. To be honest, my husband and I often cannot help but agree with her because what was the point of destroying the Soviet Union? Look at all the fighting that is going on in the former republics—blood is spilled everywhere. People suffer and who benefits? America, of course. They didn't need to go to war to destroy their number one enemy, the Soviet Union. They don't bleed. The only blood spilled is that of our brothers, the former Soviet people."

I ask her if she would want communism back and Valentina doesn't hesitate for a minute.

"They tell us now that things are different but we don't really believe it. Whoever rules, he does what he wants and the army and police back him. But at least before, we knew the rules and we were safe. Sure, some people were taken away in the middle of the night and if you were against the system you were in trouble. But now, we all fear one another.

"I believe in God," says Valentina. "My whole family always went to church, even under communism. Now, there are more churches open and that's good, and yet, despite that, people have stopped caring about each other. Under communism, we were taught to believe that the collective interest was more important than the individual. Now, it is all reversed and where does that lead us? Brother turns against brother because of money. If money becomes the

126

only reason for living, life is not worth living. Yes, I think I am for communism and collective values."

In January 1994, the Russian communist faithful were observing and honouring the seventieth anniversary of the death of the founder of the Soviet state, Vladimir Lenin. They laid wreaths and flowers at the steps of the red marble Lenin Mausoleum in Moscow's Red Square. Wreaths arrived from all over Russia bearing messages of loyalty to the communist cause, to Lenin's ideas, and to his memory. "Lenin lived, Lenin lives, and Lenin will live," were some of the messages on these floral tributes.

Millions and millions of Soviets used to make the pilgrimage to the Mausoleum and to the Central Museum of Lenin next door. Soviet culture, ideology and politics were saturated with Lenin. Lenin's portraits and words were everywhere. People waited for hours braving the cold and snow and rain to pay homage to this man. Today, the museum is closed. Lenin's body is no longer displayed and yet people keep coming.

"Lenin was my whole life. People like Lenin are rare. He devoted his entire life to the improvement of mankind. His followers, Stalin especially, deformed his ideas, but Lenin ought to be honoured by working people all over the globe," said an old woman whom I had observed laying flowers on the steps of the Mausoleum. And others, mostly elderly people whom I asked about Lenin, felt that "Lenin was a great man who saved Russia and who gave her what he had promised: land, peace and bread."

While the youth topple Lenin's statues, those of the older generation feel insulted and humiliated by the news that Lenin's days in the Mausoleum might be numbered and that his mummified corpse may be removed and buried. Clearly, even a dead symbol is still the source of inspiration to some old communists.

Many older people still feel that no matter how bad things were in the past, there was always hope that one day the world would be a better place for everyone, and that it would be the communist system, pure and undiluted, that would facilitate this development. Destruction of communist symbols makes the elderly feel as if they, personally, are being "spat upon."

Galina Ivanovna was born in 1917, the same year as the communist regime. She was a Young Pioneer (the communist children's organization), at age nine and a member of Komsomol (the communist youth organization), at age fifteen.

"I still have my Komsomol card," she says proudly.

"Communism to us meant honesty, responsibility, decency and brotherhood. We were civic-minded and we felt responsible for our motherland." Galina became a Communist Party member in 1938.

She said that people felt that something was wrong with many aspects of life then, but, she explains:

"We thought the problem was with some of the party leaders around Stalin. We didn't blame Stalin for all these strange arrests and disappearances because we thought that he didn't know about them. We didn't believe that he could be wrong."

Galina didn't lose her faith after 1956 either, when Stalin's atrocities were exposed.

"Stalin made some mistakes," she allows, "but his contribution should not be forgotten. He made the Soviet Union into a superpower. We felt proud."

In March 1994, another anniversary was observed. It was the forty-first anniversary of Joseph Stalin's death. There were red flags throughout Moscow and loudspeakers blared renditions of old Soviet military songs. As in January, there were crowds of people milling about Moscow's Red Square. Even though there is an endless flow of books and documents appearing in Russia detailing Stalin's years—the purges, secret prisons and camps, executions and numerous victims—the worship of the man that perpetuated these acts does not cease.

"Who can tell who is to blame for what went wrong with communism? Lenin? Stalin? Brezhnev? Who knows?" reflects a retired colonel whom I met at a military funeral. He was reluctant to give me his name but said he was sixty-eight years old and "a communist to the end of my days. A true communist," he emphasized.

"I think that what we observe in Russia today is a temporary phenomenon," observed the Colonel.

"It is clear that these so-called democratic forces cannot control or rule Russia. It is obvious that all the changes will lead to breakdown, chaos and economic disaster. We, the communists, made the Soviet Union a global power in every respect; they, the democrats, are destroying us. People are not stupid and they can see what's becoming more and more obvious. To regain our pride, dignity and greatness, we need communism. It's that simple. You will see, our Red Flag will fly again!"

When in July 1993, Yevgeni Yevtushenko, the most famous "rebel" poet of the sixties, walked onto the stage of the Russia Hotel in Moscow, he was greeted, as in the past, by a sold-out, enthusiastic audience. The difference between this moment and the past was that it was a celebration of Yevtushenko's sixtieth birthday and most of the audience was like Yevtushenko himself—a generation of Russians in their fifties.

Yevtushenko read his most recent poem, "Goodbye, Our Red Flag."

> Goodbye, our Red Flag.
> You were both, our enemy and friend.
> You were a comrade of soldiers in trenches,
> you were the hope of all captive Europe,
> But you also concealed from us the Gulags,
> filled with frozen bodies,
> like a Red curtain.
> Why did you do it, how could you do it,
> our Red Flag?
>
> (Translation by Marika Pruska-Carroll)

The applause was passionate because it echoed the feelings of everyone present. These were the people who first broke the spell of Stalinism following the 1956 Party Congress at which, for the first time in the thirty-nine years of the Soviet Union's existence, the excesses of Stalinism and communism were denounced. As a young poet, Yevtushenko was speaking for his generation then, protesting communist censorship and limitations upon human rights, exposing the lies and hypocrisies of the communist system and its leaders, demanding the truth and giving new hope to millions of readers. But Yevtushenko and his faithful followers never really rejected the idea of communism. They rebelled against what they perceived as the deformities and excesses of the system.

Theirs is the same generation that produced Gorbachev and Yeltsin. They do not glorify Lenin or Stalin as do Russians who are in their sixties and older. The audience listening to Yevtushenko are liberal idealists who believed, as many still do, that the communist ideology can be compatible with their dreams of human freedom, dignity, equality, brotherhood and happiness for all. This generation of communist liberals is often labelled "Khrushchev's children" because it was Khrushchev who planted the seeds of rebellion among them.

"Khrushchev's children" were in their mid-twenties when the political and cultural "thaw" started, shortly after Stalin's death in 1956. However, Khrushchev's fall in 1964 dampened their hopes and expectations. Living in the Soviet Union under Brezhnev from 1964 till 1982, they grew cynical and disillusioned. Political and economic corruption, still under the banner of communism, replaced their idealistic dreams. In the name of pragmatism, some made their compromises and resigned themselves to the surrounding realities; others were shunned and overlooked in their professional and political lives.

Then in 1985, Gorbachev, *perestroika* and *glasnost* began to unfold. All of a sudden, it seemed to this generation that their dreams were alive again. Now in their late forties, their dreams and fantasies about the "new, improved Soviet Union" were becoming a reality. "Khrushchev's children" envisioned themselves as the leaders of the new Soviet Union, a new communism where the Stalinist past would be undone, where freedom and openness would reign, and economic restrictions would be removed.

Today, almost ten years later, there is no Soviet Union and, for most of "Khrushchev's children," the dreams have evaporated. Now approaching their sixties, they admit failure.

Former rebel Nikolai, an artist nearing sixty, sums up this sentiment.

"We could not escape the past. Our history is pulling us back. We cannot accept what we see around us today in Russia, and we no longer feel we can change it. We are nostalgic for our past and the ideals that are dying along with it."

From the very beginnings of Soviet power, one of the major objectives of the new system was to create a "new Soviet man." Following the major tenets of the communist ideology, such a new type of citizen was to be committed to the collective cause and to follow the lead of the Communist Party as the "vanguard of the proletariat." Individual rights and private interests were considered secondary to the collective good, suspicious, and antithetical to communism. Private ownership was forbidden. The Soviet educational system, media, literature and every aspect of the arts were pressed into service, building and reinforcing these new social norms. The result was to be a whole new proletarian society, a new culture and social environment. Consistent with the Marxist premise that "being determines consciousness" the Soviet man emerging from this new society would be "pure" and free of any Western poison of greed and selfishness.

From the end of the 1920s until the mid-1950s when Khrushchev denounced Stalin and Stalinism, Soviet society was almost hermetically sealed from the rest of the world. History, philosophy and the sciences were reduced to a series of over-simplified truisms; the arts and literature were expected to create models of the "new" Soviet citizen. Rigidity, falsification and hypocrisy were the norm. Millions of Soviet people were subjected to this "food for mind and soul" for nearly three decades and the process of sovietization was repeatedly declared to be an enormous success.

However, while all citizens knew the ingredients for the proper "new man," very few of them became such men in their lives. Although many paid lip-service to the state's demands, the new society that emerged was not populated by the paragons of communist virtue as envisioned by the ideologues. Instead, a very specific social hybrid emerged. Reaching its cynical peak during Brezhnev's corrupt era, 1964 to 1982, this hybrid became labeled Homo sovieticus by those who studied the Soviet Union.

Not a flattering term, Homo sovieticus symbolizes the cultural and social deformities of the Soviet system. It portrays the Soviet mentality as being characterized by hypocrisy, obscurantism, suspiciousness, a lack of tolerance and closed-mindedness. It also defines the predominant attitudes toward work, exemplified by the expression, "They pretend to pay us and we pretend to work." This "work ethic" combined with the acceptance of cheating, bribing and stealing, form the legacy of communism and an integral part of the Homo sovieticus make-up.

Today, in post-communist Russia, there are few "Soviet men" but there are many examples of Homo sovieticus. They are particularly numerous among the older generations but they can be found among the younger ones as well. Consideration of Homo sovieticus in post-communist Russia is especially relevant because two of the main social issues facing Russia today are: how to determine what is and what is not Soviet in present Russian society, and how to conduct the process of desovietization.

Under communism, stealing from the state became so commonplace that not only did it not shock anyone but rather, it was perceived as being clever and enterprising. Everybody knew that "Just working hard and honestly" didn't make anybody rich, but having the right connections and knowing where and when to steal led to a "good" life. Therefore, it should not be surprising that honest and idealistic people were perceived as fools, while enterprising thieves were considered the smart ones. In the days of the Soviet Union, people used to say: "Russia is a very rich country. Everybody, from top to bottom, has been stealing from her ever since 1917 and yet, there is always something more to steal."

Ivan, a fifty-eight-year-old sociologist attempted to justify and explain their attitudes.

"What do you expect? The state took away everything from the people—their freedom and their initiative. So the people responded by taking all they could from the state, for as long as they could get away with it."

My film director friend, Leonid, pointed out that the time when Homo sovieticus came into full being was during the Brezhnev era.

"Fish rots from the head," he said.

And indeed, during this eighteen-year period, unprecedented corruption led by the communist apparatus itself, spread to virtually every social, political and economic sphere of Soviet life.

"It became quite obvious to most people that communism was dead, but we still had to pay-lip service to it and bow to its corpse," said Leonid.

"This forced double morality led to hypocrisy that became second nature to many," he added.

It is highly unlikely that someone in Russia today would describe him- or herself as Homo sovieticus, yet one finds examples of this mentality everywhere. What's interesting too is that one Russian will readily point a finger at another and label him Homo sovieticus, but practically no one ever recognizes these characteristics in himself.

Ilya, a twenty-four-year-old sociologist working happily for a joint-venture company said to me:

"Most of our people belong to the Homo sovieticus type. They exist in every age group and they represent a lot of people. I don't know if they are the majority but it is scary how many of them are around. They don't want changes. All they want is to eat, drink and sleep. They don't know anything and they don't want to know anything. They don't care whether our system is communist or democratic, nor do they really understand the difference. But they will reject anything new and unfamiliar. They knew how to cheat communism, how to get around it.

"Democracy and the free market system frighten them—communism had provided them with a minimum of security and that is all these people ever wanted. Now that nobody can guarantee such a minimum, they are against the changes."

While Ilya most emphatically disassociates himself from the Homo sovieticus type, he often displayed the intolerance and the prejudices characteristic of the type he so despised. Ilya spent six months in the United States as an exchange student. He firmly believes that "being unemployed, be it in the U.S. or Russia, is a person's own fault. Anybody who wants to work, can work."

Ilya also maintains that the "black people in America, just like our *chernota* (darkies) are lazy by nature."

Ilya had an opinion on Jews too.

"I don't think well of Jews. I am not really sure why. Maybe I believe they are manipulative. We just don't trust them. Besides, if they feel so strongly about being Jewish, why don't they go to Israel?"

It is ironic that the communist ideology which advocated internationalism so vehemently would produce results radically opposed to it—racism and nationalism. Sadly, both racist and nationalist sentiments pervade the Russian mentality and emerge during discussions on almost any subject. One can understand how the communist Homo sovieticus can embrace politicians such as the ultra-nationalist and neofascist Vladimir Zhirinovsky.

Dreams in Brown: A Talk with Vladimir Zhirinovsky

FOLLOWING THE DECEMBER 1993 parliamentary elections in Russia when the ultranationalist Liberal Democrats won the greatest percentage of votes, the Western media, particularly in North America, expressed surprise at such an outcome. I was amazed that the media were surprised. My encounters with Russians in 1992 and 1993 had well prepared me to expect this result. Such a turn-around was also predicted by Vladimir Zhirinovsky, the leader of the Liberal Democratic Party, whom I interviewed in June 1992 when only a few people were paying any attention to him.

Zhirinovsky's misnamed Liberal Democratic Party won 29 percent of the votes in Russia's first truly democratic, multi-party elections. Neo-Communists won nearly 12 percent and the Yeltsin reformers, with substantial official backing in terms of media exposure and financial support, received barely 15 percent of the vote. We may dislike the results, but we have to accept them as the product of a democratic process and as a reflection of the Russian mood.

Following the election in December 1993, I read reports that Zhirinovsky was planning to charge for interviews: $300 for the first ten minutes and $100 for every minute thereafter.

I was fortunate. I interviewed him for free before the election. I called his headquarters and asked for permission to visit him. Frankly, at the time, I was more interested in talking to the young coterie around Zhirinovsky than to the man himself, whom I perceived to be a clown, a buffoon and a crazy one, just as the Russian and Western media portrayed him. But I was also intrigued by the passion felt for Zhirinovsky by more than one of my working-class interviewees.

In the words of the poet-singer idol of Russian working-class youth, Vladimir Vysotsky: "There are too few crazy hotheads, that's why we lack mass leaders." In the opinion of some, Zhirinovsky appears to have the appeal to which the poet was referring. Vysotsky died of alcoholism in 1980 and his poems and songs, always rebellious, always labeled anti-Soviet, appealed to young Russians. Much like Jim Morrison, Vysotsky became a cult hero, opposed by the authorities when alive and even more so, after his death. Meeting at his grave took on a symbolic significance for the rebellious youth of Russia. I once interviewed a Zhirinovsky supporter who had a Vysotsky poster on the wall of his room.

I was told to come to Zhirinovsky's office the following day at 1:00 p.m. though there was no guarantee that I would see him. Upon reaching his headquarters, I was surrounded by about ten tough-looking young men. Short-cropped punk-like hair, black or brown shirts, jeans, and combat boots seemed to make up their uniform. I explained who I was and why I was there. The person with whom I had spoken the day before could not be located or identified. Clearly this was not going to be my lucky day.

But thanks to a heavy silver cross which I wear on a chain around my neck, my luck changed. An older man whom I hadn't noticed at first, walked up to me and admired my cross, saying, "It is nice to see people wearing spiritual symbols." I was too surprised to respond or to explain that, in my case, it was more a case of fashion and aesthetics. Upon learning of my quest, the man told me to wait, and disappeared only to return a minute later to tell me that Zhirinovsky would see me in half an hour and that, in the meantime, I could talk with whomever I wished.

Only then, as I began to move through the corridors, peeking into rooms crowded with people involved in pre-rally activity, did I notice that many people were wearing crosses! To my great discomfort, there were as many wearing swastikas too. Everywhere on the walls were posters of Vysotsky, along with the texts of his songs. They loved Vysotsky's songs and poems as much as I do.

At Zhirinovsky's headquarters I expected to find extreme nationalist, maybe even fascist ideas and attitudes, and I found them in abundance. What I was not prepared for was the genuine and quite overwhelming enthusiasm, devotion, and admiration that Zhirinovsky followers had for him.

The majority of the sixty or so people I observed there were young working-class men in their late teens or early twenties. There was a sprinkling of intellectuals, most of whom were in their thirties. There were only four or five older men, perhaps in their sixties, including the friendly man who helped me out. But, as one man told me, there are older supporters outside the large cities, many of them former communists. During my wanderings through Zhirinovsky's headquarters I came across only seven women, all middle-aged except for one very young woman. All were bleached blonde and busy carrying papers from one office to the next. The small number of women present in the office is a pretty accurate indication of the representation of women in Zhirinovsky's party.

The place was bursting with activity. A large Zhirinovsky rally was coming up at one of Moscow's stadiums and everybody was preparing for it. One of the younger men told me that "it is going to be hot" and he didn't think it would be a good idea for a woman to be there. When I asked him why it was going to be "hot," he said: "Some people, especially *chernota,* don't like us and we don't like them, and they like to fight and disrupt our meetings." Zhirinovsky's people, in general, were friendly and willing to talk, but wouldn't allow me to tape them. Thirty minutes passed much too quickly. I was instructed to follow the young man sent to fetch me.

Zhirinovsky's office was a large, plain room, crowded with office chairs. Behind the solid oak desk an enormous map of Russia nearly covered the entire wall. The map was Zhirinovsky's imperial vision of Russia rather than the real thing—it included all the former Soviet republics and Alaska!

I introduced myself and told Zhirinovsky that I was a Canadian academic working on a book about Russia and Russians in the midst of change, and that I was seeking answers to questions my students and friends would ask if they were in Russia and could speak the language.

Zhirinovsky is a very Slavic, and some would say, good-looking man in his late forties. He likes women and is accustomed to flirting with them. Although he wasn't my type, he has a great deal of charm and charisma and these qualities no doubt made him a successful campaigner and effective media manipulator, a factor his opponents greatly underestimated.

I asked him if I could use my tape recorder and he consented. However, after my first few questions, I was instructed to turn it off. A few minutes later I turned it on again. And so it went. I would turn it on, tape for a short while and then again he would tell me to turn it off. On a number of occasions he would ask me to make sure I taped some important comments. Throughout the interview he was quite pleasant, although I could never really figure out the criteria for what should or should not be taped.

I spent about an hour and a half with Zhirinovsky, time that later would have cost me over $ 3,000. We were not immune to the frenetic activity around us and were interrupted frequently by staff asking him questions and seeking his signature for various papers. Once, Zhirinovsky left the room for several minutes.

First, I asked him to explain the name of his party. Why the Liberal Democratic Party?

"We are all democrats in Russia now, didn't you know?" It was difficult to tell whether or not he was joking.

Sitting at his desk, he elaborated.

"I believe in a multi-party system, I believe in political competition, and I believe that the best man wins!"

"But why is it a Liberal-Democratic Party? What is the significance of the 'liberal' in the party name?"

To that he replied with a grin.

"Well, since we are all democrats, we have to add something so people can tell us apart. But seriously, we are not only for democracy; we also support reforms. But the kind of reforms we support are the kind that the people want. We do not believe in being pushed around by a bunch of self-proclaimed 'reformers' who are told what to do by the West. We also believe that people need ideas with which they can identify."

"Such as what?"

"Such as being proud of their country, of being Russian; being proud of their past, heritage and riches."

Before I was able to pursue the questioning, he waved his hand toward my recorder and said:

"Tape that. That's important. Only a year ago [he was referring to June 1991] I ran for the presidency of Russia. Of course, we didn't have political parties then, everything was still communist. There were five Communist-backed candidates, including Yeltsin, who, of course, called himself a democrat and a reformer. I was the only candidate without communist backing, calling myself what I am, an honest Russian; and I won third place just by telling the truth! You see, I believe in telling people the truth. People are not stupid and they know the truth when they hear it."

Zhirinovsky had, indeed, won an unexpected third place, capturing six million votes by promising to restore Russia's greatness and to avenge the alleged wrongs done to Russians by minorities and foreigners. If elected, he also promised to lower the price of vodka.

"I said then that Russia is heading for political and economic collapse and that the same people who were Yeltsin's fanatical supporters then, would soon enough turn to me."

The June 1991 presidential election was followed by the memorable coup of August 19, 1991. Following the coup, communism was officially declared dead. By December 1991, the Soviet Union had been officially dissolved and in January 1992, the economic "shock treatment" began. Throughout this period, Yeltsin enjoyed genuine support and enthusiasm; there were no obvious indications that Zhirinovsky's post-presidential statements were anything but the disgruntled words of a loser. Both the Russian and Western media had dismissed him as a "clown" and a "lightweight demagogue" whose "far-fetched rumblings" were not to be taken seriously.

Few would have foreseen that 774 days after the August coup attempt, where Yeltsin had defended Moscow's White House—the Russian parliament—against the hard-line communists, Yeltsin would send tanks to destroy that same White House and Parliament, which by then was no longer supporting him.

No longer burdened by an unruly Duma, in December 1993 Yeltsin announced an election for a new parliament which he assumed would support him and his reforms. But despite the official backing and Yeltsin's blessings, his reform candidates suffered a rather humiliating setback and Zhirinovsky's words rang ominously prophetic.

Everything that Zhirinovsky had told me in our interview is congruent with the statements he has made since his parliamentary victory.

"Why do your supporters wear crosses and swastikas?"

"Why do you wear a cross?" he responded. "They wear crosses because they believe in God, why else?"

"And swastikas?"

"Come on, you are an educated woman," he said. "You know that the swastika is an ancient cosmic and religious symbol and that it is also a sign of a good luck in Sanskrit. Some of our young people wear it as a sign of a good luck."

It was my turn to be indignant.

"Come on, Mr. Zhirinovsky, you know very well that the swastika was the official emblem of Nazi Germany, adopted by Hitler in 1935, and that it is still used as a symbol by fascist groups around the world!"

"Well, maybe they do. We don't."

"What is your opinion of Hitler?" I then asked.

"Hitler was a great political and cultural figure."

The expression on my face must have spoken volumes because it was then that Zhirinovsky told me to turn off the tape recorder. He then explained to me how the media tries to portray him as a fascist and that they distort every thing he says. He said that while he obviously is as outraged as any normal human being would be by the atrocities committed by Hitler and by the extremes demonstrated by fascist groups today, he nevertheless admires the way Hitler understood Germany and was able to inspire a sense of pride and heritage in Germans.

"That's the way I feel about Russia. I could fall on my knees before the Russian people. I love them so much. They have been raped repeatedly, beginning in 1917 by the communists and now again by the mafia, reformers and Westerners. I want to save them and make them proud to be Russians again."

I questioned him then about his reported anti-Semitism.

"Turn on your tape recorder now. I want it to be absolutely clear that I am not an anti-Semite. You could say I am half Jewish myself. My father was Jewish and, as a matter of fact, I was involved in Jewish activities some years back. I was once a director of a Jewish foundation but because I don't feel Jewish, I stopped these activities. In fact, I feel one hundred percent Russian. But I am anti-Zionist, and for some people in Russia, and for your Western media, this is interpreted as being anti-Semitic.

"The way I see it, you cannot be Russian and have your loyalties elsewhere—you are Russian, you speak Russian and you love your country. If you feel you are something else, Jewish or whatever, you do not belong in Russia. It is time to say out loud what should have been said a long time ago—you cannot sit on two chairs at the same time. Love it or leave it.

"At any rate, people feel much better with their own kind, with people who share their culture, traditions and heritage. Ask anyone about that. Ask yourself. In your heart, you know it is the truth. Talk to our Russian people. They will tell you how sick and tired they are of outsiders dirtying their streets and monuments. If non-Russians want to live in Russia, they have to adopt our ways, they have to respect our ways. If they can't or don't want to do that, they should leave. I don't think that is a fascist attitude. I think it is reasonable, and I think that's how most people in Russia, and probably anywhere else in the world, feel about such issues."

Pausing only to catch his breath, Zhirinovsky continued.

"It is not that I am against anybody speaking another language or practicing his own religion, whatever it may be. But if you are Russian, you cannot at the same time be Armenian or Georgian or Kazakh or Jewish or Ukrainian. That is secondary to being Russian. And, if you feel you cannot accept that, you ought to be living outside Russia."

I asked him how he felt about the disintegration of the Soviet Union and what he thought of the Commonwealth of Independent States (CIS). He had his answer ready.

"The CIS is a joke. I know it, you know it, everybody knows it. The Soviet Union will be revived. Of course it won't be Soviet but it will be Great Russia. That's what it always was and that's what it should be. Russian will be spoken from Kabul to Constantinople. It will be one great motherland for Slavs, Arabs and Turks. There will be provinces and inside the provinces, people will speak their own languages. People in the former republics don't see me or my party as their enemy. They already realize that it is in their best interest to be part of Russia. They see that this so-called independence and democracy serve only their communist rulers, who will call themselves anything to preserve their privileges. Before too long they will come begging to be part of Great Russia again."

Zhirinovsky didn't seem to be bothered by his own contradictions.

"You know that life out there is total chaos. It is bad in Russia but it is far worse in Ukraine and everywhere else. But the day will come when the bells from our Russian churches will ring from the shores of the Indian Ocean to the Mediterranean Sea, carrying messages of peace, prosperity and good will for all."

"What if the former republics don't come back 'begging'?" I ask.

"They will be back, or else. Ukraine, Kazakhstan and Belarus will return first because they have nuclear weapons and they represent a danger to the whole world and have to be controlled. If they don't come back voluntarily, they will be persuaded by military means. America should quickly realize this and not meddle. America should also stay clear of Central Asia and the Trans-caucasus or there will be Lebanons all over the place."

Early in 1994, Zhirinovsky declared that he intended to chair the new Duma's committee on foreign affairs and that he saw himself as a future Russian foreign minister for a certain period before becoming Russia's new president.

"Russia ought to be a great power again," continued Zhirinovsky.

"We are surrounded by enemies, so Russian military power is a must. I love our Russian soldiers. If they had fought under a czarist and not a communist banner, we would have won in Afghanistan. And in Europe, ultimately we will have a major say. Clinton ought to study Napoleon's and Hitler's stories and keep out of Europe. We will be number one in Europe. But above all, we need law and order."

"You sound just like the communists," I interrupted.

"No, girl, you are quite confused by your Western propaganda."

(On more than one occasion he addressed me as "girl"—at the same time flirtatious and patronizing.)

"You see," he continued, "we are the only party that matters which is not led by former communists. We are a 'third force.' We are neither former communists like Yeltsin and his bunch who changed colours and call them-selves 'reformers,' nor are we the communists, who at least have the courage to call themselves what they are. We are Russian patriots and people know it. And we represent ideas that are as old as Russia itself. Our time will come and it will be soon. The present leadership of Russia is a bunch of old communists led around by the nose by a bunch of *nomenklatura* kids who are told by America and the International Monetary Fund what to do."

Zhirinovsky was referring, in particular, to Yeltsin's former "dictator" of economic reforms and author of the economic "shock treatment," Yegor Gaidar. Gaidar, the most radical of reformers and a leader of the Yeltsin-backed Russia's Choice reform party (which won only 15 percent of votes in the recent election), comes from a famous family of prestige and privilege. His father was an Admiral of the Soviet Fleet; his grandfather was Stalin's favorite writer and one of the main proponents of the repressive socialist realism in arts and letters.

There is no question that Zhirinovsky does harbor negative feelings for "the children of privilege." The young men and women who, like Gaidar, grew up in powerful communist families, received a superior education and trips abroad, and enjoyed a lifestyle that was out of reach to ordinary Russians. Most of them call themselves democrats and reformers and still continue to enjoy a standard of living and privilege that is, more than ever, impossible for most. Zhirinovsky came out of a working-class family and had to struggle to obtain his oriental languages and law degrees, without the benefit of powerful family or communist backing. He thinks that the "democrats" and "reformers" have no links with the Russian people whatsoever and never will, and that's why they are fated to fail where he will succeed.

"America and the West should keep their advisers and their so-called aid to themselves. How much of what was supposedly given in aid to Russia, reached the Russian people?" asked Zhirinovsky.

"Nothing, absolutely nothing. Only your advisers and consultants who don't know anything about Russia or the Russian people, and our Russian mafia and *nomenlklatura* are getting rich. Our people are getting poorer every month. And don't try to tell them that they will live better in two or five years if they adopt your values and accept American supremacy. They don't believe it any more. Western aid and Western interference have got to stop. Russia is a very rich country. We have natural resources, we have skilled and well-educated people. Many countries owe Russia money. We should collect what is due to us and apply proper measures."

"Such as what?" I asked.

"First of all, we must put our Russian house in order, which means eliminating crime and mafia activities, with the aid of a strong police force; second, restore and maintain the strength of the Russian Army, giving it back its well-deserved respect and authority; and third, put people to work in enterprises that Russia really needs. We don't propose to carry on the way the communists did. We believe in reforms, in private property, and private land, but we want our Russian people to benefit from these processes, not the mafia and your Western investors.

"Russia also requires a strong leader because that's our Russian tradition. I believe I can be such a leader. Above all, I am the only leader who dares speak the truth, and people recognize this. They will become aware of it more and more as time goes by. When the time comes to vote for a new president of Russia, they will know whom to vote for, and don't you people in the West forget it."

At this point, it became clear that we had come to the end of our interview. Zhirinovsky told me to turn off the tape recorder, asked a few questions about my book and half-seriously, half-jokingly said that maybe I, for a change, would write something accurate about him and his party.

Of Cadillacs, Gypsies and Mother Russia

IT WAS A BEAUTIFUL, SUNNY JULY DAY, the kind of day when Red Square would normally be filled with Russians and tourists from all over the world. I wondered why it was closed off to pedestrians. Just like in the old days, dignitaries were being driven to and from the Kremlin in black Zhils and Cadillacs. The periphery of the historic square was lined by militiamen who wouldn't answer my questions when I asked how long the area was going to be off-limits. Then I thought this might be an opportunity to interview some militiamen, if I could just find some willing participants.

I circled around looking for young rank-and-file away from their superior officers. Luck was on my side and I persuaded two young militiamen to talk with me. They would not speak on tape but, nevertheless, I managed to get some interesting information. One of the soldiers posed for a picture with me while his partner took the photo. Such a breach of discipline would have been unthinkable in the old Soviet days. There were no other militiamen in the

A heavily-decorated Afghanistan veteran. Veterans who served in that country were not allowed to march in the Victory Day parade, May 8, 1995, in Moscow.

A Russian soldier with English patches on his uniform.

immediate vicinity and from a distance, it looked as if a female tourist with a camera was flirting with two young men on duty, with one of them politely giving in to a request for a picture.

"You know these Western tourists" my two young militiamen could say to a superior officer, if reprimanded. "She just wanted her picture taken on Red Square."

The men were twenty-two and twenty-three years old. They thought it was a good thing that the Soviet Union had fallen apart, but they also believed that Russia was like a "mother to all the former republics" and like Zhirinovsky, they believed that the "republics will all come back to Russia because that's the way it always was and, as anybody can see, the republics can't manage by themselves anyway."

They didn't like Gorbachev and they didn't like Yeltsin—"Russia needs a strong leader and it will be somebody who will restore law and order." I asked them whether it meant returning to a totalitarian system and they were quite shocked that I could even think that.

"Communism is dead and that's why we don't care for the old guys like Gorbachev or Yeltsin. Guys like them cannot make a difference because deep down they are communists. They are no different from that monster who started it all."

"What monster?" I wanted to know.

"Lenin, the one we are still guarding. All the communists who followed him were monsters as well."

When I asked who they thought could become Russia's new, strong leader, they could not think of any specific person. But when I asked them whether they thought Zhirinovsky could be such a man, they nodded. "Yes, Zhirinovsky is a good Russian, not a communist or a democrat, and he has some very good ideas on how to handle *chernota*. Yes, he probably is the only man in Russia who could do it."

"He would have to get rid of all these mamma's boys like Gaidar and the rest, because all they know is how to dance to the American tune. The way for Russia is not the way it is in America or anywhere else in the West. Russia is different and Russians need their own, different ways. Zhirinovsky understands this, although at forty-eight he is not that young himself. Eventually it will be up to us, the youth, to change things. But he is better for Russia than anyone else."

Our brief exchange was over and the pictures came out nicely.

My encounter with two young street vendors the next day was not planned. I was walking down Manezhnaya Ulica, one of Moscow's main streets, when suddenly I was surrounded by a group of about ten Gypsies, mostly children, I think, though there were two men in the group and perhaps three women. The children began to pull at my carrying bag and my pockets while at the same time pushing me. I was completely taken by surprise, though I ought to have known better. Both Russians and foreigners had warned me about these incidents on Moscow streets.

It took me a few moments to regain my wits and then I started screaming, kicking and pushing. This, and my unexpected cursing in fluent Russian caused them to pause long enough for me to push through them and run. I grabbed two young men who were standing nearby and demanded help. They didn't seem surprised and placed me between them. A few other people on the street stopped to look and the Gypsies disappeared.

It turned out that nothing had been stolen. The zipper on my bag was half open and one pocket of my jacket had been cut but tape recorder, camera, money and everything else were still in my possession. The attackers hadn't had enough time to finish their work. It seems that as much as they had surprised me, I had surprised them as well.

I thanked my defenders and, naturally, began to talk with them. They were students, nineteen and twenty years old, who became street vendors, selling anything and everything they could buy and sell, as they put it. They were just leaving their post to get more merchandise when I ran up to them.

"So, how do you like our *chernota?*" they asked.

"You have to be really careful because they are very well organized and they know their job. They took you for a foreigner, American or something."

I told my defenders that I was Polish (I have a Polish accent in Russian which comes in handy because a Pole is not considered quite the foreigner a Westerner is). In the few minutes we had to talk, they managed to tell me how much they hated everything that is happening to Russia. They don't see much point in studying. They survive by "just peddling things." They detest both Gorbachev and Yeltsin and blame them for destroying everything.

"Before, Russia was a great power and now we feel like we are a nation of beggars."

They were not interested in politics or any political leaders. It was the summer of 1993 and they hadn't heard of Zhirinovsky then. Now who hasn't? But I wouldn't be at all surprised if they voted for him.

Natasha is twenty-two years old and studies physics. Oksana is twenty-one and studies chemistry at Moscow University. I met them on a bus going to the university when I asked for directions (one of my ways of starting conversations with people). We began to talk.

"Look around you in the streets," said Katya.

"It can be Moscow, or St. Petersburg. You see people trading everywhere. All our towns and cities have became one great market place. And where they trade, they drink and fight. You see so much hate, aggression and fear everywhere now. And most of these people are *chernota*. We don't discriminate against them; they seem to have a special talent for commerce but we really don't want them in Russia. They bring violence, dirt and noise with their goods. The *chernota* should not be permitted here. That's what Yeltsin and his capitalism have brought us."

I asked them what they thought could be done about it. They looked at each other and then Oksana made a suggestion.

"If you get the chance, go to Zhirinovsky's rally. He has good ideas on what to do. Russia should be for Russians."

Lena Petrovna is sixty-two years old and a retired clerk. To survive, she buys small, light-weight items like tea, matches and pepper in the state stores and sells them for five times the state price outside the store. It's a common way for the elderly to supplement their pensions. Needless to say, if one wanted to buy these items in the store itself, it would be necessary to wait for hours, and even then risk not being able to buy them because of frequent shortages. Lena is profoundly unhappy about Russia's state of affairs. She thinks it is a tragedy that the Soviet Union disintegrated.

"They sold us out to the West. Gorbachev, Yeltsin and all these reformers. We were strong, we were important, and we lived decently. We had law and order. Communism was better. Anything would be better than what we have now."

"Is there anybody that you trust in Russia today?" I asked.

"Yes, there is one man. His name is Zhirinovsky and he said that he would get rid of *chernota* and crime. He ran for President of Russia; did you hear of him?" she asked. "You see, it is the *chernota* who are messing up Russia. Moscow is dirty and dangerous because of them. I don't know how it could be allowed. Men, women, children! Begging, stealing, drinking, fighting, destroying our streets and monuments. It is all *chernota* and they have bags full of money!"

Valentina Osipovna, a fifty- six-year-old retired cook, also had bitter words about what she saw around her:

"They are everywhere. You can hardly get into the metro; you can hardly walk through some streets, they are selling, selling and selling. They will sell their own mother."

"Who are 'they'?" I interrupted.

"Oh, they are *chernota,* of course! It is bad, so bad. Look how filthy, how smelly, how dangerous our cities have become. They have taken over all of Moscow. There ought to be some restrictions, some laws against it. They should clean up after themselves. But no they leave such dirt, such, mess. It is simply a shame. I am a native Muscovite and my heart aches when I see what they do to my city. I am shocked. The *chernota* brought fear, frustration and crime with them. Sure, I know our Russian people can also be bad. They can also rob and steal and kill. But nothing like these *chernota* people. Oh no, nothing like that.

"The worst of all are the Caucasians and their clans. They have whole wars going on between different clans. They shoot each other and they shoot our people. They look like dirt, they smell even worse but they are millionaires! It has to be stopped!"

"Who is going to stop it?" I asked.

"I don't know much about politics and such but whoever gets rid of *chernota* and crime will get my vote."

Valentina Osipovna didn't know of Zhirinovsky or his party when I talked with her in the summer of 1993, but she virtually repeated his words about Russia's need for pride and greatness.

"It is a shame that our great Russia has fallen apart. Who has benefited from giving up all this international prestige and importance? Only our enemies. We belong together. They (the former republics) need us. For centuries they were part of great Mother Russia. We need the prestige back. We need strength, pride and respect. And we will have it back. Of that, I am sure!"

But What about Democracy, Ilya?

WHEN THE BLOODY "DISSOLUTION" of the Russian Parliament took place at the beginning of October 1993 and hundreds of people were killed and thousands wounded, the event was acclaimed by Yeltsin and his supporters as "a victory of democratic forces over the hard-liners."

Many Russians who did not support Yeltsin, did not condemn him either. "If the enemy does not surrender, you kill the enemy," were the famous words of the Russian writer, Maxim Gorky, supposedly offered as advice to Stalin in the early 1930s. A few years later, Gorky himself was eliminated. Democracy, Russian-style?

These days, democracy is a tarnished word in Russia. For Vera, a recently-married twenty-two-year-old history student, it is a very confusing concept.

"If we at least *had* this so-called democracy. With all the talk about how free and democratic we now are, we are neither free nor democratic. We are not free because our people are not tolerant of anything or anybody that is different; we are afraid of being different. And we are not democratic because we don't even know what democratic means. I don't think we are going to be free or democratic anytime soon."

Marina is a twenty-seven-year-old lawyer, working for the Moscow City Council. She is married with no children. Marina feels that "to talk about capitalism and democracy at this time is a gross misunderstanding. It will take more than one generation to accomplish it, just as it took four generations to establish communism."

Twenty-four-year-old Ilya, his brother Grisha, and his parents, Tatyana and Ivan, were some of the people I have met repeatedly over the past three years in Russia. Three years ago, Ilya spent a semester in the United States as an exchange student.

"My concept of democracy developed when I was in America," says Ilya. "In my opinion, democracy means strict enforcement of laws which ensure the welfare and freedom for all people in society. And," he continues, "freedom is a general term and I don't want to speak about it because it is not an empirical term. The relationship between democracy and freedom is theoretical. There is freedom in the United States and in Canada. In Russia we have complete freedom now, but we do not have democracy. Freedom ought to be controlled

The author in front of the restored White House, no longer the seat
of the Russian parliament. It is presently being used as heavily-guarded
government offices. The building was seriously damaged by the attack
ordered by Yeltsin in October 1993.

or it becomes chaos or anarchy. Uncontrolled freedom is not a positive thing. No democracy is possible where there is uncontrolled freedom. There ought to be strict laws and they should be observed."

I made a point of getting in touch with Ilya following Yeltin's attack on the Russian Parliament. Not surprisingly, Ilya was supportive, if not fully enthusiastic about Yeltsin's actions.

"Democracy means observing and understanding laws. There was too much freedom in Russia and Yeltsin put an end to it."

When I suggested to Ilya that Yeltsin's method was not necessarily constitutional or in accordance with the law, he dismissed my point.

"I certainly prefer it the way it is now to what it was before October," he said.

"Of course, we will have new elections and a new Constitution, and we need both. Most people my age don't feel the way I do. They really do not care about these issues. And most of the older people prefer law and order, and it does not matter to them who institutes these or in what way."

Ilya and his family all represent different points of view and, more than once, only half-joking, one family member would say, "If there was a civil war in Russia today, we would be fighting one another."

"Our people are suspicious and sceptical when they hear the word 'democracy' these days," says Ilya's father, Ivan. "All they want is law and order, and it appears that they might get some degree of that."

I spoke to Ivan after October's events as well, and he said that basically the events changed very little in terms of people's attitudes.

"People still think of democracy as something synonymous with lawlessness. And if they approve, however grudgingly, of Yeltsin, it is not because they think he is a democrat, but because he showed strength in dealing with the opposition. Strength is respected in Russia. I personally tend to think that the traditional Russian form of governing with a strong sense of authority, works the best for us."

Ivan provided me with figures indicating the mood and attitudes of the people. His Sociological Institute conducted a national public opinion poll in June 1994 which found that 42 percent of all Russians wanted strong authoritarian power. Ivan believes that this percentage is even higher now.

However, the same poll indicated that 88 percent of Russians are not interested in politics at all. Yet, only six months earlier, following the events of

October, 51 percent of those eligible to vote went to the polls. (This figure is in striking contrast to Soviet-style elections of not so long ago, when the turnout was almost 100 percent because eligible voters were expected to vote.) These people decided to give politics another chance and voted in the December elections. After the election, polls indicated that people who voted then, did so to show that they were either for or against Yeltsin. But, and this is interesting, all those who voted, regardless of whether they declared themselves communists or democrats were for law and order. Also, most of the voters declared that the choices were unsatisfactory and that the end result was unlikely to improve their lives.

Clearly, the members of Ivan's family do not differ on this issue. His older son, Grisha, a thirty-year-old factory worker and the only family member without a university education, has no use for concepts such as democracy or freedom. For him, it is all Western hogwash that destroyed the Soviet Union and that now is destroying Russia.

But Grisha is for law and order and he is very enthusiastic about Zhirinovsky's Liberal Democratic Party.

Grisha and Ilya have very intense arguments about politics. The law and order issue is the only one upon which they agree. Grisha says that his way of thinking is very popular among his fellow workers. He calls his brother Ilya "a sold-out democratic traitor" and his father "a wishy-washy communist." But he sees himself as, above all, "a Russian patriot."

Lala, a woman in her mid-thirties, a lecturer of English literature at Moscow University and mother of two young children, thinks that "all this talk about freedom and democracy is a lie." Her husband, Boris, in his mid-forties, is a former councillor of the Moscow City Council which was dissolved by Yeltsin in October 1993. He was very bitter at the time of the Council's dissolution, and remains so today. When he was elected to the Council in 1989, he was so enthusiastic about the changes brought by *perestroika* that he wanted to devote his life to working for them. Only five years later, Boris's thinking has changed dramatically.

"Democracy, privatization, reforms—everybody has had more than enough of it. I don't see anything constructive taking place. It is sad because people invested so much of themselves for change. They thought, we thought, that once the communists are out, everything would change, that there would be hope. That hope died shortly after the August 1991 coup. People don't believe in change any more because they see that the people who are in power now are stealing and grabbing all they can and that it happens at every level."

Retired cook Valentina thinks that democracy is the problem.

"I don't know much about such things," she says, "but I do know when things do not work."

Valentina claims that she was "cautiously optimistic" when Gorbachev introduced *perestroika* and *glasnost,* but now, she says "for people of my generation, all these changes are a total disaster.

"True," says Valentina, "we have freedom now and people are no longer afraid and that's very important and good, of course. We can hear things on the radio and TV now that before, we would not dare say to a close friend."

But Valentina also feels cheated and confused by all the new information she is bombarded with.

"We cannot get used to the idea that everything we grew up with was bad—Lenin, the Party, communism."

Leonid, the film director, and his wife, a famous film star, have two sons, aged seventeen and nine. Leonid, in true filmmaker fashion, presents me with a picture.

"I just observed a woman in St. Petersburg involved in a spontaneous political street scene. A crowd had gathered on the street waiting for a grocery store to open up. Everybody was complaining about the shortage of butter. One woman's voice rose above the crowd, 'Who cares about the butter? We need freedom, not butter!' This woman who shouted is dearer to me than the whole chanting crowd. 'Freedom, democracy!' Do you understand? The Bolsheviks didn't succeed in killing her spirit. She didn't sell her yearning for freedom in return for a little security. The Bolsheviks almost killed the Russian spirit. The real issue today is how much of this spiritual strength is still alive within Russians."

Bulat, who is involved with a Canadian business firm in a Canadian Russian joint venture, is a new type of Russian. He is a businessman and proud of it. Bulat speaks fluent English, has visited both Canada and the United States and, while he is all in favor of a free market economy, considers himself a political pragmatist and is critical of Yeltsin. Bulat has a wife "to take care of me and the baby," lots of money, and strong opinions.

"Democracy and freedom as they are understood in the West are not applicable in Russia," he says.

"Russia, as you know, has no tradition of democracy, and it probably will not be democratic in the near future."

Bulat, who reads the Western press on a daily basis, laughs at the depiction of Yeltsin as "a democrat."

"What we will have in Russia for the next twenty or thirty years—that is if we are lucky and if the world does not blow itself up sooner—is a political model that is uniquely Russian. It will be a mixture of hard-line rulers applying modified communist methods, calling themselves democrats, enforcing law and order, exploiting nationalist sentiments and relaxing economic controls. And that's fine with me."

When I ask if he thinks such a model will appeal to the majority of Russians, Bulat observes that it will probably be "the only truly democratic wish of the people" expressed in actual voting for a political party that will clearly represent such a platform.

"Russia is not able to deal with democracy; it has not the slightest undertstanding of democracy. That's the major difference between us and the West and it will always be that way," concludes Bulat.

When I spoke with him in the summer of 1994, he told me that he was becoming more and more cynical every day.

"Democracy is hardly a topic of concern to Russians. Human rights or justice do not exist. Mafia and government—and one is not sure where one ends and the other begins—make a mockery of it all. There is a total disregard for the law. I no longer believe there can ever be democracy in Russia."

Will the Real Democrat Please Stand Up!

EVERYONE IN RUSSIA has an opinion when it comes to Gorbachev and Yeltsin. What comes as a great surprise to Westerners is that Russians have a much more positive view of Boris Yeltsin than of Mikhail Gorbachev. Westerners don't seem to grasp that the Russian views of these two leaders are influenced as much by recent developments as they are by hundreds of years of Russian history characterized by autocratic rule. Democracy is an unfamiliar, foreign concept, often with sinister implications of chaos and anarchy, and, for many Russians, the name of Gorbachev is synonymous with democracy. On the

A small town's main street with pre-revolutionary buildings built of wood,
disintegrating, but still heavily used. The horse and cart is passing a shop
selling "industrial goods"—the equivalent of a hardware store in the West,
although you might find it selling anything and everything.

Relaxing with friends—like in the old days when life was familiar and
old age secure. Such serenity is only possible in small towns.

other hand, Yeltsin is perceived as a "strong man" and a "fighter." In Russian political culture, a strong leader suggests law and order and, not far behind, autocracy, something known and familiar to all Russians.

Members of the Russian intelligentsia tend to be much more positive about Gorbachev than less educated Russians, who almost unanimously reject Gorbachev. Younger people, more often than not, dismiss both politicians as personalities linked with the past rather than the future.

Serafina Piotrovna, who works in a bookstore on Tverskaya Street, Moscow's wide and drab main street near Red Square, is sixty years old. She used to be an elementary school teacher, then worked in the library until her retirement. Barely able to survive on her pension, she decided to capitalize on her friendship with the store manager and got a part-time job working at the bookstore.

Serafina is short and grey, one of the countless *babushka* one sees everywhere in Russia. An intelligent and well-read woman, she doesn't have kind words for either Gorbachev or Yeltsin.

"Gorbachev started the process of disintegration of the Soviet Union," she says. "And Yeltsin is in the process of destroying Russia."

Leonid does not have too many kind words for Yeltsin either, though he is definitely anti-communist, pro-democracy and pro-reforms. Leonid and I have talked on a number of occasions over the past three years, as well as just after the armed attack on the Duma in October 1993.

"Today, the Bolsheviks are in power more than ever, no matter what they call themselves. They still have the number-one boss who calls the shots; that's Yeltsin for the moment, and he and his group disregard all laws. Their so-called governance is a huge improvisation from one moment to the next. Every aspect of our lives is dominated by Yeltsin and his clique. It is the same with the free market reforms, privatization and everything else. Yeltsin orders it and Yeltsin runs it."

Leonid most emphatically distinguishes himself from those who blame Gorbachev for Russia's dire situation.

"You know, judgements and accusations will not create a new system," he says.

"But the one thing which is absolutely necessary is the Russians' obligation to give Gorbachev his due. Russians who say that he 'destroyed' the Soviet Union forget the circumstances under which he began his *perestroika*."

Leonid launches into a lengthy discourse describing Soviet realities preceding Gorbachev's ascent to power in 1985, then says:

"Gorbachev's wisdom was demonstrated in the small steps he took in his domestic policy. Outside the Soviet Union, in foreign policy, he took giant steps because he knew what to expect from the West and he knew what Russia needed. Inside the Soviet Union, he knew of the many hidden perils. He waded into completely untested waters. But his strength was in the small steps and gradual changes. He started as a communist and he was moving, albeit slowly, toward democracy.

"But think about it! When we look at all those modest initiatives taken between 1985 to 1991, we see that Gorbachev accomplished giant historical leaps—he freed Eastern Europe from communism and he unified Germany; in Russia he made it possible for the people to speak freely and not be afraid.

"And yet, all of a sudden, there appeared this army of dyed-in-the-wool democrats, led by Yeltsin, who started accusing him of not going fast enough!

"I believe that the disintegration of the Soviet empire was a perfectly logical process and that it would have taken place sooner or later. However, Gorbachev was trying to slow down the process, to soften the blow. The 'democrats' would not let him. They were calling for bigger, faster steps. We got them; you see the results."

Valentina claims no knowledge or understanding of politics or economics. She emphatically states that she will not talk about politics or politicians. Instead, during our two-hour ride on a crowded train, she talks about her daughter and grandchildren. But inevitably the names of Gorbachev and Yeltsin come up.

"I wouldn't want things to go back to the way they were before Gorbachev, although before Gorbachev, at least we knew what to expect," she says.

"I think Gorbachev had some good ideas but he got corrupted by Western ways. It's his fault that the Soviet Union collapsed. We are all paying for it now.

"Yeltsin is better because he is for law and order. He should issue more decrees and get rid of all these troublemakers who disagree with him."

I spoke with Valentina in the summer of 1993. The following October, Yeltsin did what she was hoping for. There are many Russians who think and feel as Valentina does.

Andrei, who is thirty-eight years old and works as a chemical engineer in a factory on the outskirts of Moscow, was initially enthusiastic about the reforms and Gorbachev. Then he became disenchanted and sincerely believed Yeltsin when he accused Gorbachev of stalling. After the coup of August 1991, Andrei felt very optimistic about the future. Today, he is utterly disgusted with Russian politics.

"I was so unfair in my quick negative judgement of Gorbachev and my unconditional support for Yeltsin. Unfortunately, there are many of us who did exactly the same thing.

"Gorbachev gave us freedom of expression, and we, the intelligentsia, rejected him. He freed Eastern Europe; he ended the Cold War; he got us out of Afghanistan; and above all, he started the process of destroying that cursed system, communism! And we rejected him! We decided he wasn't moving fast enough. Imagine!"

"And what has Yeltsin done for Russia? What are his wonderful deeds? His reforms made paupers out of nearly all of us. The mafia has made millions of dollars. Russian blood has been spilled. The KGB is stronger than ever and they and Yeltsin are the staunchest of allies. And worst of all, the people are beginning to take the communists seriously again."

Bulat is an ardent supporter of reforms but claims that politics do not interest him. He wants a capitalist Russia with maximum flexibility in the economy and a minimum in politics. To put it simply, he is making a lot of money and he wants to be able to make more.

"Gorbachev will be judged fairly by future generations. Right now, he is detested by Russians and respected by Westerners," says Bulat.

"Most Russians do not understand Gorbachev because basically he is a Western-style reformer and speaks a language that is foreign to us. We don't really know what freedom or democracy are and how they relate to our lives.

"Yeltsin, on the other hand, is perceived as 'the man of the people.' And these 'people,' the majority, think with their emotions and not with their heads. That does not translate into political knowledge or experience.

"When Yeltsin speaks, you can hear how plain and simple his ideas are. People like those ideas because they think they understand them. But Gorbachev is a real intellectual and that was his major strength and his major weakness. The ordinary people did not understand him and they didn't trust him."

Bulat believes that Yeltsin's crudeness and a certain awkwardness endear him to the Russian people. They see him as a fighter and not a "tricky egghead." And the rumors about his drinking and womanizing reinforce his macho image held so dearly by many Russians.

Yeltsin's dissolution of the Duma makes his image as a strong leader that much more pronounced. It is this image rather than that of a democrat, that will help Yeltsin remain in power in Russia, Bulat believes.

Gorbachev impressed twenty-seven-year-old lawyer Marina.

"Perestroika and Gorbachev were very important in my life. I was nineteen when it all started and I was drunk with happiness. I thought all our dreams were coming true. And Gorbachev was my absolute hero!"

Marina then frowns and says with great sadness and cynicism:

"All dreams die. I was very naive then. Now, I don't believe in anything much. The Soviet Union fell apart and Gorbachev caused it to happen, willingly or not. And now Russia might perish. I doubt that Yeltsin will get us out of this political and economic mess. Everybody lives in great fear of tomorrow. Soon, there will be some great national tragedy and Russians will turn against Russians if we continue this way."

My friend Ivan with whom I spoke every time I traveled to Russia over the past three years, said to me last summer:

"I think perestroika was an immensely important process and, until the 1991 coup, I was a very strong supporter of Gorbachev. But after Gorbachev, perestroika lost its meaning. Gorbachev had a vision and the people who succeeded him, people like Yeltsin and his circle, haven't the drive, talent or knowledge to carry on with this vision."

Ivan believes that Gorbachev's principal error was that he didn't address economic issues first. He thinks that the Chinese way would have been preferable for Russia. "Gorbachev should have started with the economy, then we could have begun to build everything else."

Ivan did vote for Yeltsin in June 1991 when Yeltsin was elected President of Russia.

"I didn't vote so much for Yeltsin as I voted against the methods that were used by the hard-line communists to get rid of Yeltsin. Let's not forget that the Communist Party was still in charge then," Ivan adds.

"I voted against dishonesty in politics. But Yeltsin's variety of democracy turns out to be very close to autocracy and, even worse, is leading nowhere."

Ivan informs me that the public opinion poll done by his institute in

February 1992 indicated that 42 percent of all Russians wanted a strong authoritarian power.

"All that most of our people want is law and order. A political leader who will deliver this goal will have lasting power. It might well be Yeltsin."

Ilya, Ivan's entrepreneur son doesn't agree.

"I am all for reforms but I am not too happy about Yeltsin's and Gaidar's shock treatment type of reforms or the present situation. There is too much talk and not enough real action. Besides, I just don't care about politics and politicians. Whether it was Gorbachev or Yeltsin, it really doesn't matter that much, because they both were former communists.

"I wonder whether the transition from communism to democracy or whatever they choose to call it, is even possible."

Ilya shrugs his shoulders when I try to point out that Gorbachev's *glasnost* and *perestroika* resulted in unprecedented freedom of expression never before known in Russia, and that it was a radical transformation of the Soviet Union.

"What you people in the West don't understand is that for most of us in the former Soviet Union, life before Gorbachev and *glasnost* and *perestroika*, was not the kind of barbed wire communist horror story you seem to think it was.

"You imagine we lived in constant terror, afraid of the secret police, not able to do anything. Well, it just wasn't so. Ordinary people lived like people everywhere else do. They worked, they dreamed, they loved, they hoped for a new apartment, a car, a trip abroad. Most of them never had anything to do with the police, labour camps or political persecutions.

"Also, the majority of people are not writers or artists, deprived of creative freedoms. Most people just live their ordinary lives. And most of our people never even heard about the dissidents that you knew about, nor did they care.

"Of course, their lives were difficult, but the difficulties were related to shortages of consumer goods, to crowded apartments, to drinking spouses and not to politics or political fears.

"For most, politics or dissidents and their concerns were things that were alien. People worked, dated, made babies, drank, lived and died. And I am sure that most people over thirty today would prefer life the way it was before Gorbachev. I know that my parents would. It's not that they prefer communism, but the majority of people prefer to have familiar problems, familiar shortcomings and a general sense of being taken care of by the state, which, they felt, was strong, powerful and respected by the world. So, are you surprised that they don't care for Gorbachev and his reforms?"

I press on and ask Ilya whether he feels that way too.

"I won't have communism back in my life in any form. But I do not feel that today's politicians speak for me either. In the future, we will create a new generation of politicians. And they will represent me."

When I spoke with Sasha, Volodya and Genya, eighteen-and nineteen-year-old Moscow University chemistry students, they echoed Ilya's sentiments. They didn't care about Gorbachev.

"He was a communist, like all of those old men. He probably didn't even have a plan or a policy."

They believed that the freedom which emerged as a result of *glasnost* and *perestroika* was a by-product of processes that had gotten out of hand and that it was neither planned nor intended to go as far as it did.

Most of the group of eighteen female Moscow University students with whom I met in the summer of 1993, were about ten years old in 1985 when *perestroika* had started. They expressed a wide range of opinions about Gorbachev and Yeltsin.

"Gorbachev finished communism!"

"I thought *perestroika* was a lie right from the beginning."

"Gorbachev destroyed the Soviet Union!"

"No! He helped it to fall apart because it was all held together by fear and force."

"I believed he was a true democrat. Now I am not so sure."

"I don't care for any politics. With Yeltsin, we now have another dictatorship. Is that all there is for us?"

"I think history will be kinder to Gorbachev than we are now, but he hurt us too much; he destroyed all our values."

"Speak for yourself! Not my values."

"But Gorbachev will be remembered and Yeltsin will not."

"Gorbachev and Yeltsin represent our parents. They do not represent us."

Two young soldiers in their early twenties, on day-leave in Moscow, were quite outspoken in their assessment of Russia's political transformation while we chatted over a beer. Politicians were given short shrift too.

"Gorbachev and Yeltsin lost touch with Russian people. They both are communists at heart and cannot be trusted. But communism is dead.

"What Russia needs is law and order and a free market economy. The way for Russia is not the way it is for the West. Russia and Russians are different. Gorbachev listened to the West too much. But Yeltsin and his bunch cannot really make a difference in the long run because they belong to the generation of Communist *apparatchiks*. It is not they who will shape the future. It will be us," they emphatically stated.

A few days later, two teenage punks whom I approached in front of a Moscow music store that sells the latest in heavy metal, were not interested in talking about politics but wanted some questions of their own answered about Western grunge bands, and other rock groups and personalities. We agreed to trade information. In a nutshell, they gave me their view of politics and politicians.

"To hell with Gorbachev! To hell with Yeltsin! We have freedom now! We can make money, we can get rich! We can have things that people in the West have, we can listen to our music! That's what human rights are all about! Democracy? Who gives a damn!"

Economic Paradoxes

IN RUSSIA TODAY, nothing is what it seems to be. One enters a bakery and finds whisky, perfume, and condoms instead of bread. One goes to a meat market and finds fish. It is impossible to buy cheese or honey in regular grocery stores, but you can purchase any brand of American cigarettes. There are no matches to be found in Moscow but on every street corner one can buy Bic lighters. You can find a head of half-rotten cabbage selling for about five cents, next to kiwi fruit costing a dollar each. With his monthly pension a pensioner could buy forty kiwis.

On the main streets of Moscow and St. Petersburg one has no problem locating the boutiques of Dior, Chanel, Nina Ricci, and other famous designers, where the cheapest item costs more than a hundred dollars. And right outside these well-guarded stores are beggars in rags.

On city streets Cadillacs, Porsches, even Rolls Royces are juxtaposed with noisy Russian-made vehicles belching exhaust. It's perfectly normal to have Russian customers, most of them young, arriving at car dealerships with suitcases full of money to purchase cars worth fifty to a hundred thousand dollars.

There are restaurants which are expensive even by Western standards, where you can eat only if you have an American Express card. Even in fast-food outlets like Pizza Hut, one pizza, a salad, two beers and coke, cost $40. I was shocked when the bill arrived. In any of Moscow's hotels where Westerners stay and pay $360 dollars a night, a cup of coffee costs five dollars.

I was once taken by a Russian entrepreneur friend to a nightclub where the annual membership fee is $10,000. There are quite a few such clubs in Moscow and it is considered normal to spend $500 or more in one evening. To enter a club, even the moneyed elite have to be frisked and pass through a metal detector. Heavily-armed men are in evidence both inside and outside these clubs and restaurants. Some of them are bodyguards accompanying patrons while others are club staff. Nearby, in stark contrast, pensioners and homeless children beg for spare change and forage in garbage bins.

Looking as if they have emerged from years of war and deprivation, Russian cities and towns are crumbling. Broken windows, boarded doorways, streets and alleys with potholes and garbage replace the once spotless sidewalks.

In a 1994 report, Moscow was declared to be the world's third most expensive city next to Tokyo and Osaka. St. Petersburg was not far behind. The Swiss Corporate Resources Group, a company used by international firms to calculate living expenses for their workers abroad, compared 155 goods and services worldwide.

Dangerous paradoxes are evident everywhere in Russia's economic life. Cash-strapped nuclear power plants can't afford to pay their workers, and safety enforcement is deteriorating in all sectors. Russia's eight major nuclear power plants produce over 10 percent of the country's power but are not being paid for the power they have already supplied. As a result, they are dramatically in debt. Nuclear plant workers repeatedly picket the ministry in Moscow, demanding back pay and safety measures.

"The plants are operating in a continuous emergency situation," both plant managers and union representatives are quoted as saying in the newspapers. "It is impossible; we are on the brink. The workers are in a ugly mood and, God forbid, something terrible can happen."

The output of Russia's crude oil, its "liquid gold" fell dramatically in 1994 due to a drop in demand. There are fewer and fewer paying customers. Fuel and Energy Ministry enterprises are owed a total of about nine billion dollars. Among the debtors are former Soviet Republics, and in Russia, huge metallurgical plants, farmers and the whole military-industrial complex.

Shopping in a small town is simple. Usually there is only one store in town,
with very little on its shelves. Customers wait patiently outside while the
store is closed for lunch.

Back to the Soil

IN RECENT YEARS many Russians have moved away from the cities. Those with relatives in the countryside have gone to live in small towns and villages in an attempt to live off the land. There are no numbers or statistics to indicate how widespread these relocations are because it is still a relatively new phenomenon, but people are certainly talking about it. Almost everybody knows someone who has made such a move. I was told of people seeking the less hectic, more subdued lifestyle of Russia's provinces: workers—white collar and blue collar— who lost their jobs and couldn't get new work; parents with young children fearing for their safety in the big cities; and many simply fed up with both the pollution and crime prevalent in urban areas. It is said that whole new communities are forming in different regions of Russia, composed mostly of the intelligentsia, former students, and other city folk disenchanted with the reforms and Russian-style democracy.

Other city dwellers spend their weekends at their cottages in the country. But it would be a mistake to think they go there to relax after their work week in the city. The whole family works—growing potatoes, cabbage and other vegetables on the small plots surrounding their cottages. More often than not, the cottages themselves are hardly more than unheated huts without electricity or running water. Many of the teachers, professors, engineers and other professionals I have met are engaged in intensive weekend farming to make ends meet. Some city people spend their free time working alongside relatives who live in villages not far from the city, for a share of the produce they grow.

I became friends with Nadia, a forty-year-old woman who was a clerk in a gift store where I shopped. One Saturday morning she invited me to accompany her on her regular trip to her relatives living in the village of Golubka, forty-five kilometers south of Moscow. She told me that most families could not feed themselves without such help from the countryside.

According to Nadia, regardless of the fact that stores were full of goods, much of the food grown in Russia was still in short supply. One never knows whether you are going to find such staples as flour, buckwheat, salt or sugar.

"So," she said, "people still hoard things. You worry about being hungry so you feel safer if you have a fifty kilo sack of each at home."

Unfortunately, as she told me later, food kept for a long time attracts insects and rodents and large amounts of the hoarded goods have to be thrown away. Potatoes and cabbages rot before they are eaten.

"And yet," continues Nadia, "that's our psychology; we are afraid to be caught unprepared—what if there is a civil war or something?"

"Also, one has a good feeling working with the soil. Russia has so much land. Nobody should ever go hungry. Before, under communism, people wanted to escape to the cities. Life in the country was so terribly hard. Now it seems that our only security, our only safety, is being close to the soil."

When I asked her whether her relatives living in the village also felt this way, she said I should talk with them myself.

I followed Nadia's advice and found them very reluctant to speak. Certainly not on tape. But after a day of making myself useful working with the family, they relaxed a bit.

Nadia's relatives no longer lived in the *kolkhoz* where they spent most of their lives. Fifty-five-year-old Danill and his wife Varvara, who was around the same age, lived in a small two-room house with a big kitchen and no bathroom. It had electricity but no hot water. Eventually they bought an acre of land surrounding the house. They were joined by their thirty-three-year-old son, Andrei, recently laid off his job at Moscow's Zhil car factory, and his wife, twenty-nine-year-old Lena, with their nine-year-old son. They all live now in this small house, one family in each room.

Andrei and Lena rent their two-room Moscow apartment for the equivalent of $150 per month. It is more than what Andrei was making at the factory. They work on what they like to call "their farm." They are making ends meet but encounter many problems. They have difficulty obtaining seed, fertilizer and equipment. They resent the fact that there is no attempt made by the local authorities to help individual farmers. And the peasants, especially ones still working in the *kolkhoz,* are very hostile.

"But" says Danill, "whatever city folk will or won't do, we will not go hungry. We can feed ourselves."

Russian agriculture is in chaos. During 1994, Russian production of meat and milk dropped twice. Imported farm products are not only cheaper but also do not spoil because many contain preservatives and the Russian consumer prefers them to Russian produce. As long as there are virtually no tariffs on foreign food products, the Russian farmer is paying the price. The situation is not made any easier by the lack of storage facilities, transportation, packaging and market outlets for Russian products. All these factors render Russian agricultural products uncompetitive with imports.

Nadia's family's situation is far from typical. At least she and her family have managed to purchase their piece of land. Most other peasants do not have the money to do so. There are still many peasants who are absolutely horrified with the idea of private ownership of land. They tenaciously hold on to their collective farms and resist any change. They feel that being a member of the *kolkhoz* provides a certain minimum of security without the uncertainties of private ownership.

Nobody trusts the central authorities. Danill told me that the peasants feel that "Moscow has washed their hands of any responsibility" to them and they have every reason to be mistrustful. As long as government does not provide proper credits and a protection from imports, "private farming for profit will be impossible."

Doing Business

BULAT IS THE RUSSIAN GENERAL DIRECTOR of a Canadia-owned company that studies the impact of oil exploration on the environment. Bulat, who is thirty-seven, has held this position for five years. He is pleased with his high salary which is paid in U.S. dollars and he is happy with the degree of independence he is given. He is less happy with daily Russian realities.

Any foreign company that wishes to do oil exploration in Russia has to have formal approval of the International Finance Corporation and a permit from the Russian Ministry of Environment. In order to obtain both the approval and permit, the project must be proven to be environmentally sound. Specific concerns must be studied and all possible negative effects have to be identified.

Bulat's company prepares such studies. With a staff of five office workers doing administrative work, he hires consultants, Russian and foreign, for specific projects. He is quick to admit that the work does not always proceed smoothly. There are frequent attempts to influence the outcome of specific studies. However, in general, it is in the interest of a company wishing to engage in oil exploration to know all the facts beforehand and not be caught damaging the environment at some later point. This is more obvious to the Western companies than it is to the fewer Russian outfits.

When the consultants complete their studies they make recommendations to the future oil exploration companies. Once the company is approved by the authorities and issued a permit, it may choose to ignore the recommendations and risk being caught later on. The environmental damage that occurs results from poor monitoring once the exploration process has started.

I asked Bulat to describe the climate for business in Russia. He began by criticizing the corporate taxation system.

"Taxes are absolutely crazy. It is a joke, except it is not funny. Nobody but nobody could make a profit if he paid taxes as expected," he says. "If you pay taxes, you are left with nothing."

"So, what do you do?" I ask.

"You cannot be legal," answers Bulat matter-of-factly.

"I don't see any reason to pay taxes. They only go to support the lifestyle of those in power. Nothing comes back to society—it is robbery, plain and simple. It is every citizen's duty to evade taxes, because the money one pays goes to private pockets and out of the country. It is immoral to pay taxes in today's Russia."

Bulat doesn't expect any changes soon. Paying the taxes or trying to evade them, costs money. But there are other stumbling blocks, namely the mafia.

"Today it is virtually impossible to be a successful businessman in Russia without attracting the mafia's attention. Every business arranges a special bank account for payoffs just in case."

"Do you pay the mafia?" I naively ask.

"Would I tell you if I did?" he answers.

Despite the adversity involved in being an independent businessman, Bulat is doing well. He works hard and admits to having few interests outside his work and family. He used to be interested in theatre, good books, and culture in general. These pastimes are no longer part of his life.

"There is no time for it and, frankly, I just don't care for all this spiritual and intellectual stuff the way I used to," he admits. But, overall, Bulat is rather pleased with life and is cautiously optimistic about the future:

"Before, under the communists, there was nothing. Empty shelves and no opportunities. We were all drowning in mediocrity. But today, people have something to strive for. It is true that the majority of people are unhappy and they are not able to buy all the goods that are available now. It is also true that we have great differences in standards of living but I believe the situation now is more natural. There ought to be differences because people do differ. Some are more able than others and ought to be rewarded. The free market system rewards ability, independence, creativity and hard work. I'm all for it."

"But what about the future?" I press him.

"I hope," says Bulat, "that the economy will normalize somehow. While it is a fact that the mafias control the economy right now, hopefully one mafia will prevail over the others and instill some kind of order."

If Bulat doesn't even mention the government as an agent for order, it is because, as he puts it, "one does not know anymore where government ends and the mafia begins, or the other way around."

He is pessimistic in the short term but optimistic about the future because he believes that "the market will take care of itself, it will prevail and, in the long run, everything else will follow."

When I question how long that may take, Bulat states that "it will not be long—maybe ten, fifteen years."

The Zil Car Factory

VALENTIN MET ME at the Avtozavodskaya metro stop—literally, the "auto-factory" station. The station marks a kingdom of sorts—an immense district which includes some 400,000 people whose lives for the past sixty years centred around the Zil Automobile Factory.

Valentin, fifty-seven, an imposing figure with a shock of white hair, could not be missed. I recognized him without a moment's hesitation though we had never met. He still is the chief technological manager of this giant car plant that once employed 120,000 and still employs over 60,000 men and women. Not for much longer however. Zil was privatized in 1992 when it became a joint venture with Caterpillar Inc. The plant still faces cash flow problems and it was forced to cut production in half in 1994. There will be further layoffs and reductions. The only question is when.

Valentin drives a Russian-made Moskvich. It is a smaller and cheaper car than the famous Zil that his factory has produced for decades. Zils were traditionally the car of choice of Communist Party *apparatchiks* and still used by the present power brokers.

Besides limousines, the factory manufactures trucks. However, there is no longer a great demand for either vehicle.

"It is not that Russia does not need trucks or limousines any more," explains Valentin, "there seems to be more need for limousines in our new democracy than ever before, but our new 'democratic' masters prefer Western ones. As for the trucks, we produced inferior trucks and our whole technology is geared toward a continuation of such production. Nobody needs or wants them any more. We used to sell them to the former Soviet republics. This market no longer exists."

For three hours Valentin generously drove me around the "kingdom of Zil," giving me a tour of the factory and surrounding facilities that, literally, addressed virtually every aspect of company life. We stopped and talked to different groups of workers, young and old, men and women. The experience was not a cheerful one.

Before the advent of *perestroika* in 1985, life in the Avtozavodsky district was familiar, safe and predictable. Practically all the workers and their families lived in the apartments that surround the plant. Apartments were subsidized by the factory and it was considered a very good deal to work for Zil. They took good care of their people.

The average family of four would occupy a three-room apartment for which they would pay only a token rent—a situation considerably more fortunate than that for other Muscovites. Whether the workers will be able to retain these apartments and the preferential rents for much longer is anybody's guess.

Workers were cared for by the factory's medical facilities without cost. They still are, but the quality of care has disintegrated. Their children went to the factory's nursery and kindergarten. During the summer there were free vacations for children and the families. Jobs were guaranteed for life, and after three years of maternity leave, women could return to the same positions they held before. Workers have already been warned that it won't be long before these benefits will be taken away.

Valentin spent his whole life in the area. He came to work in the factory when he was twenty-three years old. His father was a skilled worker there as well. His wife, now retired, worked in the factory's cultural centre.

The cultural centre is located in a beautiful park. A palace-like structure, it houses a theatre, a concert hall, a cinema and a library. Opposite the park is an enormous sports centre which includes a football stadium, a huge swimming pool and various track and field facilities.

They stand mostly empty now because the factory no longer receives subsidies from the state to maintain the facilities and to carry on the activities.

"Vandalism is everywhere now," says Valentin. "Before, life centred around these places. The memories of my whole life are here. I had a wonderful childhood. Now, everything is dying.

"In the cinema, sometimes American movies are shown. One must pay to get in and some private 'businessman' sells alcohol to our young people. That's our 'culture' now."

"What do people do now when they aren't working?" I ask.

Valentin shows me. Clusters of men sit drinking in the park, or doing the same on street corners.

"They don't do anything. They drink the cheapest, often dangerous vodka, they beat their wives and children, and they vandalize the facilities they were once proud of."

Valentin, so far, was lucky. He still had his job and apartment, and his children are educated and employed. He hopes that he and his wife will be able to survive on their pensions when the time comes.

The workers that I spoke to during the tour of the factory were uniformly negative about the changes taking place in Russian society, cynical about their political leaders, pessimistic about their own prospects and worried that, despite its joint-venture status, the factory might close nevertheless.

"If they close us down now, that's the end. Where shall we go? What shall we do?" That was the uniform response from the older workers; the younger ones didn't want to talk about it.

I asked Valentin whether he personally had anything positive to say about the changes. His answer was somewhat unexpected in the context of his overall nostalgia for the past.

"The communist system created for us a small, secure, but isolated world. But the big world, the real world outside, was closed to us. There was security and small comforts and rewards, but there was no freedom. One would always be rewarded for playing it safe. Initiative was viewed with a suspicion. We are all paying for it now.

"I will never forgive the system for depriving me of seeing the world. I never traveled. Ironically now that I have the freedom to travel, I don't have the means to do it and I know that I never will. That's my greatest regret in life. I haven't seen the world."

A number of younger workers who lost their jobs at the car factory have found occasional jobs in private house construction. Apparently, many of Moscow's nouveau riche are building houses. They pay well and, since it is a new type of work, they hire people who will learn on the job. There were few private houses built in Russia during the communist years and there are few skilled workers experienced in single-home construction. According to Valentin, the amount of money spent on these private mansions is incredible and nobody is asking questions about where the money comes from. These *businessmeny*, as they call themselves, spend a lot of time in the company of various political figures.

"Watching such characters and their affluence," says Valentin, "teaches our young that only people like that get places in today's Russia. They look at their own parents, who worked hard their whole lives and they see that they are going under. The mafia types are becoming the role models for our youth."

Valentin does not think that young people in his factory are interested in politics. "People are obsessed with survival now," he says.

"My mother used to say, 'If it is bad, it will get worse before it gets better.' I think she was right. Our people expect the worst. They can see that the rich get richer and the poor get poorer. And, of course, the major problem in Russia is that we do not have anybody in the middle."

Valentin is not optimistic.

"I understand the need for change. But I am unhappy because now I can see that these changes will not happen within the next few years. It will take more like twenty or thirty years to change our mentality, our work ethic. Meanwhile, there is no program, there are no laws and I fear that eventually we will end with a free-market economy and a dictatorship worse than anything we ever knew."

Bread or Clean Air?

I MET SERGEI totally by chance. He was visiting Moscow and I met him at a friend's home. Sergei is involved with the Russian Green movement that had its beginnings during Gorbachev's *perestroika* in the mid-1980s. While Sergei was very enthusiastic and optimistic about saving the environment five years ago, he is pessimistic about it now. I was told by my friends that Sergei, a thirty-seven-year-old doctor, is probably one of the best-informed environmental specialists in all of Russia. He lives in Magnitogorsk, a city behind the Ural mountains. When he learned about my book, he volunteered to tell me the story of Magnitogorsk.

Magnitogorsk was the most famous industrial centre of the Soviet Union, and it maintains its preeminent status in today's Russia. Following Stalin's ascent to power in 1928 and his massive five-year development and industrialization plan, the decision was made to locate Magnitogorsk close to rich iron ore veins. In the course of just a few months, a rail line was built, linking the new city with the Trans-Siberian line. Fifteen thousand workers were brought from all over the Soviet Union to Magnitogorsk and in 1932 the steel mills began operating.

Sergei described to me how the city, the steel mills and the factories grew. Young communists from all over the Soviet Union volunteered to work under extremely harsh conditions. Sergei's grandfather went to Magnitogorsk in 1930. His father was born in 1932. Both were committed communists building the model communist city.

Along with the communist volunteers, over 40,000 workers were serving sentences in Stalin's forced labour camps. During the 1930s Magnitogorsk became a symbol of the "victorious communist industrialization."

Presently there are 80,000 people working in Magnitogork's steel mills and factories. The factories produce most of Russia's tanks and other military equipment. The city has a population of nearly one million people.

Magnitogorsk also produces some 600 tons of pollutants each year. Sergei says that during the last ten years, the number of cancer related deaths grew 30 percent among women and twelve percent among men. The number of stillbirths is climbing; the present rate is 20 per one thousand births.

In 1985, Sergei and his colleagues were receiving growing support for their research documenting environmental destruction.

"We had a great deal of support then, but now we have very little," he said.

"Magnitogorsk is one of the few places in Russia where industrial production is not slowing down. Apparently, tanks and other weapons are still in great demand. Our people still have relatively secure jobs, subsidized housing, and a number of benefits that they were receiving under communism. Even though they know now that they are paying a big price for the security and benefits, they are not willing to compromise. Environmental safeguards cost a lot of money and are not obtainable along with full employment. Our people know it. During the local elections, they choose the candidates who promised them jobs and rejected ones that were committed to clean air."

Sergei told me that not all workers who work in Ural region factories are as "fortunate" as the workers from Magnitogorsk. A number of Siberian factories that produced non-military items had to reduce the number of workers and limit or eliminate benefits. Some factories had to close altogether. Many factories have switched to four-day work weeks, others have forced workers to take "vacations" with only minimal pay. Subsidies that once paid all-encompassing benefits, are now shrinking day by day. Many workers are not receiving back pay owed to them. Sergei does not believe that these factories will ever be viable again.

"They produced items that are no longer needed. There are no markets for them. Eventually, people will leave. Where they will go, I don't know. There are fewer smokestacks now and less pollution, but people are very unhappy and they all look with envy toward Magnitogorsk with its killer pollution and its tanks. Less pollution and fewer jobs also means a dramatic increase in crime, alcoholism, drug addiction, rape and virtually every form of violence against people and property. The police are no longer able to control local crime; there are more and more homeless people, especially among the elderly, and more and more people think of the past as a time of 'glory and happiness.'"

PART FOUR

Ten Years Later:

Russia's Youth in 2002

Russian youth have embraced aspects of Western popular
culture—its music above all.

The Generation Gap: Russian Youth
and the Prospects of Democracy

IN SEVERAL VISITS TO RUSSIA after the turn of the millennium, I discovered a growing mood of confrontation between the generations. All over Western Europe one hears that the demands of a flood of elderly pensioners is eroding the foundations of the state. So it is in Russia: it is said that by 2030 one in three Russians will belong to *stariki,* the over-fifty generation, and will need to be supported by the other two working men and women.

And their numbers are shrinking. Between 1990 and 2000, the population changed from 150 million to 142 million, a loss of eight million.

The verbal duals between the generations are growing more heated. The tradition of respect for the elderly is being replaced by the Western cult of youth. Not so long ago, the older generation dictated their offsprings' choice of lifestyle, profession and even marriage partner. The only way a young person could gain prestige and authority was to wait. Today, however, the older people are being pushed to the margins of society.

A few years ago it was unthinkable for a young person to sit while an elderly person stood on a bus or in the subway. Today, it is more likely that only an old person will stand up for someone even older. The young tend to ignore their elders and, at worst, they abuse and insult them. Life experience does not count for much in a society where knowledge becomes dated faster than clothes. Listening to the young gives one the sense that the older people never knew anything useful. Besides, "the old ones are guilty of installing, supporting, defending and deforming" communism.

Russians over thirty refer to the young as "play-kids" whose motto seems to be "Let's go faster. Let's play!" The older generations seem to be slowing down the game by holding jobs the young want, and exercising caution the young detest.

There are major differences between Russia and the West, however. While Western baby boomers and pensioners are relatively wealthy, healthy and powerful, most of their Russian counterparts are poor, sick, and defeated. Nevertheless, they are still numerous enough to make a difference at election time, and unlike the young, they have political views and they vote. They are like the older generations in the West in being ready and willing to exercise civic rights and responsibilities. While the oldest among them are dying rather rapidly in Russia, all over the world they are becoming a larger proportion of the total population and their political convictions and their awareness of their rights and responsibilities will have a dramatic impact. The young are afraid that the result will be the "dominance of demography over democracy".

Youth, Political Values and Democracy

OVER THE PAST DECADE in Russia the régime, the institutions, the élite, and the system of official political values have all undergone radical change. A new generation has appeared, and its understanding of politics will be based on objectives and orientations that are different from those of their parents. The development of Russian democracy will depend on this new generation and their values.

The development of the civic personality occurs under the influence of the prevailing political environment, which is made up of agents of socialization including such conditioning elements as the family, peer group, school, religion, art, culture and mass media. They channel basic personal orientations toward authority, conflict and order, violence and tolerance, and freedom and discipline.

Under communism, there was a single, rigidly dogmatic set of political values. Today, collectivism is a thing of the past. Diversity of views is "in".

Massive re-socialization has been underway in Russia. In ten years, the Russians have been challenged to learn new political standards and a new political vocabulary. They are struggling to forge a new political consciousness and new political behaviour to be able to assert their vital interests in the fast-evolving political sphere.

My conversations with and observations of young Russians, ages fifteen to twenty-five, elicited strong reactions. These are the people whose primary political socialization coincided with the years of *perestroika*. My sample was limited to 100 young urban Russians. The emphasis was on discovering qualitative trends. (This will be treated more fully in a forthcoming book about Russian youth.)

Regardless of their precise age, everyone in my sample group thinks of "big politics" as boring. Their knowledge of politics is abstract. The younger they are, the more they associate success with the ability to conform.

They understand democracy as a "law-governed state." The Yeltsin régime was perceived as weak and not democratic, and Putin's government, in their eyes, represents an improvement in terms of both democracy and strength. However, civic responsibility and participation in state affairs are low on the list of democratic values that they embrace.

Contradictions abound. For example, while there is a lack of interest in politics, some of the young people expressed a desire to become an elected politician—a kind of political opportunism. Most of my respondents consider it acceptable for a minority to govern a majority. They have no problem with social inequalities. My respondents said they obey the law, but they reflect no clear understanding of it, nor do they wish to understand how political authority operates. Their perception of politics is emotional: they feel sympathy for institutions such as parliament, but they do not trust them. I observed a definite correlation between the respondents' ages and their interest in politics; the younger they are, the less interested they seem.

Russia's Hip Teenage World

I WAS TALKING WITH NATASHA, a Moscow teenager. We had arranged to meet in a downtown bar called Quasar, a popular hangout. Most of the patrons were high school seniors. It was dingy, crowded and smoky, and smelled awful. The walls were plastered with posters advertising Western beer and soft drinks. The noise both upstairs and in the basement was deafening, with techno music everybody seemed to love.

Natasha and her friends sat on bar stools or strolled around. They smoked all the time. They loved to show off their six-inch platform shoes, bell bottom pants and skimpy tops. They drank an occasional Coke, 7-Up or beer. Natasha was skinny and tall, with the mandatory long, straight, streaked blond hair. The girls were clones of each other. Mine was the only face definitely over thirty. I got a shocked look every few minutes when somebody new walked by. "It's okay. She is from Canada," Natasha would reassure her friends.

Natasha's parents are friends of mine. They would not dream of going to

Quasar. No adults wandered in. I was "invited" to talk, but it became obvious that nobody could talk here, so I decided to observe and to get a feel of the place. I hoped to get some kids to agree to meet with me later. I succeeded in getting twelve of them to meet me later in a nearby park where I would tape two hours of rather passionate conversation.

Sitting on a bar stool trying to look cool in my own platform shoes and bell-bottoms, I observed how little the patrons differed from European or North American teenagers. They seemed to adopt even the minutest detail. Moving through the haze and loud music were teenagers dressed in wacky shoes and hobo clothes, with nail polish ranging from yellow to the popular black. The girls were wearing their hair long and straight, while the boys' heads were shaved.

They love to watch American movies and they are crazy about American movie idols, as well as Western music and MTV. They talked about drugs and sex and either wish to indulge in both, or do. Computer games are part of their lives. There are computers in Quasar. For the equivalent of a few dollars you can use them. You can also play a game of Laser Tag for three dollars.

This is a lot of money in a country where pensioners have to survive on $65 a month. I made a note to explore how these kids came into possession of money, knowing that their parents often have to make do on $150 per month.

Quasar is managed by a Briton named Guy Barlow. Like many other bars and restaurants in Moscow, it is owned by Westerners. These businesses are profitable because the young Muscovites are consumers. They want Western culture, and they want it now.

Teenagers are the key targets of Western advertising. They believe it. Even people in their twenties show considerably more scepticism and caution when bombarded by the same ads. I am sure that within a few years these teenagers will develop a healthy resistance to advertising, but for now they embrace it totally, without reservation.

Both the teens and the twenty-somethings profess a preference for Western products. They share a belief that a product's price reflects its value. They don't go bargain-hunting. If you bought it cheap, it must be worthless. A story was circulating while I was in Moscow. Two Russians meet on the street. One says to the other, "Your leather jacket is great! How much did you pay for it?" The other replies, "$200." "Where did you get it?" "On Arbat Street." "You fool! You could get the same jacket on Maneazhna Street for $500."

Paying more is associated with higher status. Teenagers will brag about how much they paid for something, upping the actual price. To impress your friends, you buy and display an expensive brand.

However, the patrons of Quasar, one of the "in" hangouts while I was in Moscow but no doubt soon to be displaced by another grungy teenage bar, are not representative of the majority of Moscow teenagers. They are, however, the most visible, and they are quite defensive about their visibility. One of Natasha's friends told me that they see themselves as "the bravest." While they are convinced that other kids would love to look and act like them, they admit to being harassed or laughed at sometimes by their peers. "They are jealous. They cannot afford to be like us or they don't dare," explained Natasha.

Her crowd, I found out later, is not interested in politics. They did not know and do not remember the communist past. Born in the 1980s, they were too young to associate deprivation with communism. That makes them radically different from their older siblings. People in their twenties have different associations. The naïve faith of Natasha and her teenage friends will probably evaporate as they move into their twenties.

The teenagers are just as puzzling to the twenty-and thirty-somethings as they are to their parents. Misha, a thirty-two-year-old business executive, told me he cannot understand them at all. This sounded odd, because he is a marketing professional responsible for producing advertising for jeans for the teenage market.

"My generation," he said, "was 'against'. We knew we were against the communist régime when we were teenagers. These kids don't reject anything. They grab anything and everything. Western clothes, movies, music, culture— they want it all, without discrimination or distinction. They eat it up! They are consumers, and that's all they are."

Russia's Youth and the New Markets

IT IS CLEAR that the very young in Russia today have priorities and loyalties that are different from those of previous generations. In the not-so-distant past the Communist party shaped the mindset of Russian youth. Today, it is marketing executives. Western and local Russian business are fighting intensely for market share and brand loyalty.

The goal is to capture the minds and imaginations of the young. The young in Russia, those sixteen to twenty-five years of age, constitute more than 35 percent of the country's population. They are growing up surrounded by ever-increasing Western-style consumerism, something that seems foreign and often repugnant to their parents and grandparents. They act like their Western counterparts. They recognize brand names and they are eager to try the products. Apparently they have the money—there are even indications that they are spending more than their Western peers. It is still the case that Russian subsidizes housing, health-care and education, leaving Russians with more money, proportionately, for luxuries. Young Russians are, moreover, more likely than Westerners to continue living with parents who provide them with the basics.

A typical "young Russian" as defined in a national survey by a Russian market research company, is a twenty-four-year-old single, living with his or her parents, with a university education, and earning the equivalent in rubles of about $800 a month. That is a dramatic difference from his or her parents, who may also be university educated, but bring in about $300 a month. Of course, this group of "typical" young Russians is quite small, about six percent of the total population. They live in Moscow, St. Petersburg, or other cities. They are precisely the people who will have the greatest impact on Russia's future. This group spends approximately 80 percent of its income on items other than basic necessities. They are different from young people in the country and small towns, but they are even more different from the other generations right in their own homes. In economic terms, young people in Russia are more independent than they have ever been.

The Western companies that are most visible in Moscow today are mostly those described as "fast-moving consumer goods makers." They produce soft drinks (Coca-Cola, Pepsi-Cola, 7-Up and Sprite are popular) and fast foods (Pizza Hut, McDonald's) and candy bars (Mars, Snickers and hundreds of other brands).

Alcohol and tobacco companies can market to Russian youth without the restrictions they experience in Western countries. Everything is permitted, including distribution of free samples of alcoholic drinks and cigarettes. As in the West, marketing in Russia equates consumer products with fun. Companies sponsor popular events, usually sports or music, and organize special promotions. Some TV commercials are identical to those geared to Western markets; others are specifically addressed to young Russians. MTV-inspired advertising is proving to be as successful in Russia as elsewhere. A Pepsi campaign with the Spice Girls, not originally intended for Russia, turned out to be immensely successful there.

There is enormous growth in disco clubs in the cities and the outlying regions and international companies use them to set up promotional activities. Sprite affiliates itself with teenage fashion and music magazines, for example, and distributes a CD of its jingles mixed with dance music. Its main rival, 7-Up, has taken advantage of the craze for in-line skating and several years ago began sponsoring an annual competition in that sport in Moscow. Pepsi capitalizes on the Russians' love of soccer by sponsoring the new Russian premier soccer league, targeting a slightly older segment of the young crowd.

Promotional give-aways work well for cigarette marketers. Russians have long been heavy smokers. That is an unfortunate common denominator among all the generations. Despite evidence of the harm it causes, smoking is a growth market in Russia, replacing lost tobacco revenues in the health-conscious West. In Russia, tobacco companies sponsor music and sports events, distribute freebies, advertise on billboards, and print their logos on sports clothes and accessories purchased by the young. Thousands of teenagers get their first puff of tobacco at sports events or concerts where pretty girls offer them free cigarettes. Smoking Marlboros, Pall Malls or Camels is perceived by the young as cool and sophisticated.

Young Russians and Computers

ANOTHER GAP IN RUSSIAN SOCIETY today is related to rural or small town versus big-city. Between them, Moscow and St. Petersburg have some 15 million people, ten percent of all the Russians. Moscow especially seems to be another country. The two cities are easily twenty years, or a generation, ahead of the rest of Russia. This applies to every sphere of life, but it is most apparent in the area of computer literacy.

According to a July 2001 survey by *Internet Monitor* reported by *Kommersant Daily*, one of Russia's most influential papers, Russian Internet users are more educated than other European surfers, with 69 percent of Russians having higher education, compared to 48 percent of the Europeans. Russian surfers are also more likely to have travelled abroad and have higher income. The survey found that on average the Russian user goes online for 49 minutes at a time and that most began to use the Internet in the last two years. There are eighteen personal computers for every thousand people. (In the U.S. there are 565 computers per thousand people.) Eighty percent of Russian personal computer owners live in Moscow and St. Petersburg.

There are few computers in the countryside or the small towns, but in many places where they are visible, they are hardly ever used. I have seen bank tellers in Nizhnyj Novgorod, a medium-size city in Central Russia (population about 1 million), doing calculations on a computer and then double-checking them on an abacus. The abacus is very much in evidence in banks, stores and post-offices, even in Moscow.

Outside of the business people who use computers and the owners of PCs, computers are viewed as gadgets from another planet. Few Russians over forty are comfortable with them. The younger people are more likely to be computer users. They may not own one, but they may have access to them at any of the private schools their parents are paying for. Internet cafés are slowly beginning to appear everywhere. These youngsters speak English or some other Western language and use computers with the same ease as do the young in Western Europe and North America. Most of the young, affluent residents of Moscow and St. Petersburg are sophisticated computer users. But the young who are not affluent or a resident of these two cities, are also more likely to use computers.

It is forever being pointed out that one of Russia's greatest assets was and is its highly educated population. However, people were not exposed to the computer on a large scale until the mid-eighties during Gorbachev's *perestroika*. In post-communist Russia massive educational programs for things like computer literacy are no longer provided or subsidized by the state. During the twilight of the Soviet Union, only a select group of young political, scientific and military aces became immersed in computer culture. President Putin, who is in his forties, belongs to this group.

Putin's computer skills led to an international incident. During the first year of his presidency, he met with other leaders at the Group of Eight summit in Japan. He suggested that they communicate by e-mail. Most of the others had no idea how to use computers. Some couldn't tell the difference between a mouse and a keyboard.

At the turn of the millennium only 2.2 million Russians were using the

A moment in front of a cosmetics store.
Although there have been many changes in contemporary Russia,
women are still reponsible for the shopping—just like in Soviet days.

Western companies that are most visible in Moscow today are producers of consumer products: Soft drinks (Coca-Cola, Pepsi-Cola, 7-Up), fast foods (Pizza Hut, McDonald's) and candy bars (Mars, Snickers and hundreds of other brands).

Internet. The number is growing: in 2003 it is expected that ten percent of the population will be online.

Online sales "are set to explode," according to investment company Brunswick Warburg. It is predicted that within the next three years e-commerce will hit $900 million. Russia's e-revolution may have an impact matching that of the Bolshevik revolution of 1917.

As of 2002, however, only four percent of households had computers, compared with 28 percent in Western Europe. Ordinary phone lines in Russia are poor quality and scarce, and credit cards are nearly non-existent. But the price of a personal computer is falling, as is Internet access, and Brunswick Warburg predicts that about 13 million private homes will get computers in the coming year.

Mobile phone sales are rising even faster than computer sales. Perhaps mobile phones will become the main Internet access point for Russians.

Russia itself gives even more dramatic figures. According to *Russian Internet Monitor* (IV) in 1999, 5.4 million Russians over eighteen were using the Internet. The average age of Internet users was thirty-one. According to the report, 18 million Russians get information from the Internet, either directly or from friends who are direct users. Even this report agrees that most of the users, whether they own a PC or have access to one, are people living in Moscow or St. Petersburg.

The dramatic change in the educational system over the past decade is a factor in computer use. "You get what you pay for" is now the catch phrase. The more affluent parents in the two affluent cities send their children to expensive private schools where they learn computer skills, foreign languages and business skills. Virtually all these children own a PC.

Russians traditionally respected education and in seventy-five years of communism there was not such a disparity as now exists. Programs across the former Soviet Union were remarkably uniform. It didn't matter much where one went to elementary or high school; there may have been a greater variety of teachers in Moscow, but the textbooks and curriculum were the same everywhere and the school was free. State grammar and high schools are still free of charge, but the best teachers are in the private schools, which have a different curriculum. Private schools exist only in St. Petersburg and Moscow. Their existence has set in place a growing great divide, the reversal of a long process. Sound mass education is being replaced by a high quality education for a narrow elite, and an inferior education for most. The profile of Russian society has started changing, rapidly and radically. The older, educated, large segment of the population is dying, with the loss of its skills and potential. This is particularly the case of scientists. They are getting out of touch with their disciplines and experience a sense of being devalued and under-appreciated. Younger Russians can no longer take for granted that they will receive the standard quality education that their parents and grandparents got.

Nevertheless, the computer is penetrating everywhere in Russia. In *In Siberia* (1999) Colin Thubron tells of an encounter in the Khabarovsk, a city of 600,000 on the Chinese border 300 miles south of Vladivostok. Thubron met a woman who told him about her daughter. "My daughter is twenty. She went somewhere in Khabarovsk and bought herself an e-mail connection. She now gets information from abroad. E-mail! I hardly dared to buy a stamp. But she and her friends see things differently."

I also met a number of young people living in towns outside Moscow and St. Petersburg who buy e-mail connections and use what may be the town's only computer in the local coffee house. They connect with the world and are part of the global village. This fact alone has greater implications than almost anything else.

In Place of a Conclusion

RUSSIA IS CHANGING every day. There is no conclusion. Instead, there are glaring paradoxes evident everywhere. Since the eighteenth century, led by Peter the Great, Russia and her so-called enlightened elite strove to emulate Western models and standards. But they most often succeeded in transforming these models and standards into the exact opposite of themselves. The results were uniquely Russian! It is most likely that this tradition will continue and Russia's future will represent an unpredictable hybrid of Russian traditions and Western influences.

MEMBRE DE SCABRINI MEDIA

Québec, Canada
2003